Illinois Central College
Learning Resource Center

SPEECH
in
the classroom

Donald H. Ecroyd
Associate Professor of Speech
Michigan State University

Prentice-Hall, Inc.
Englewood Cliffs, N. J.

19270

PN
4121
.E3

Current printing (last digit):
12 11 10 9 8 7 6 5 4

Preface

In the classroom, to teach is to talk and to learn is to listen. The classroom, in other words, is full of oral interaction, whether the subject be mathematics, French, or second grade spelling. Every classroom teacher is a speech teacher whether he wants to be or not, for learning, listening, teaching, and talking cannot be separated.

This book is directed to the teacher in training. Its aim is really two-fold. First, it is designed to help develop those speaking skills which are so much a part of the teacher's daily professional work. Second, it is planned to give insight into the kinds of speech problems that elementary and secondary students face. To his students, and to himself as well, every teacher owes his best possible communication skill.

Although I personally prefer to teach the materials of the course for which this text is intended in the order suggested by the chapter arrangement I have used, there are certainly other possibilities. For example, the course could be begun with the study of Chapter 5, on materials and their arrangement. Or one could easily bring the last three chapters to the beginning of the course. Some of my friends and colleagues suggested that I arrange my chapters in one or another of these ways on the philosophic grounds that the first of these orders would begin the course with analysis of *thought* rather than delivery, or that the second would make the course "start with the student." Personally, I prefer to commence with the *voice* because I feel that this is the area in which students have their greatest insecurity and in which they have had the least previous instruction. I have left the last section till the end in the belief that these matters have always seemed easier for me to teach when the students before me have already developed some fundamental awareness of how they can improve their speech—an awareness developed as they observed the improvements they made themselves.

iv PREFACE

Another way of organizing the course would be to relate certain chapters in Section One directly with the activity-centered chapters in Section Two. For examples, Chapters 1, 2, and 3, on voice, diction, and general expressiveness, could be tied in with Chapter 6, on oral reading. Chapter 4, on posture and gestures, could be added when you move on to the activity of story-telling, and so on.

Your own teaching preferences and the needs of your students can and should dictate such matters, however. The book is organized to be used as it is, but it is also deliberately structured to make adjustments possible.

I am grateful to the Alabama Education Association for its kind permission for me to use portions of my article, "Let's Talk It Over," as a basis for parts of Chapter 14. The article, which appeared in the *Alabama School Journal* of October, 1954 (Vol. 72, No. 2), was itself a re-working of a speech delivered to the Alabama Speech Association.

I also want to thank my mother for her drawings, which, I feel, add much to the clarity of the text.

DONALD H. ECROYD

Contents

section one

Fundamentals of effective speech

Experts do not completely agree on the nature of the "fundamentals of speech." However, no one disputes that some considerations are basic to all studies of oral communication, serving in a sense as common denominators of all speaking. Among them are our voice, diction, vocal variety or expressiveness, and our general appearance and bodily action. Even more fundamental than these matters of delivery are the soundness and proper arrangement of those things of which we speak.

These are aspects of speech which we must repeatedly consider, both as teachers and as speakers. They are basic in all that we do ourselves as talking teachers and in much that we have our students do. Whether our goal is the immediate one of self-improvement or the eventual one of improving others, we need competence and awareness in these matters.

1

The voice

The voice is a unique and sensitive instrument. Consider, for example, the fact that you can pick out the voice of someone you know in a large choir, or the fact that you can say the single word, *Oh!* to express almost every known emotion. Every voice is different. Even upon so limited a reproducing instrument as the telephone you can recognize almost without exception the voices of your friends. Every voice is capable of a wide range of expression, varying from the calming tones of a mother at her baby's bedtime to the shrill crescendo shriek of the cheerleader at a big game.

How does this miraculous voice of ours work? We do not yet know the whole story, although we can give you some understanding of the process of phonation.

As a teacher you will need to know something of how the voice is produced in order to be able

3

to use your own voice to the best of your ability. You are judged
by your voice. It is one of the principal ways by which you show
the world what your personality is like. As a teacher you also need
to understand the basis of good vocal production in order that you
can help, rather than harm, your own students in the developing
of their speech patterns. The ability to speak clearly and interestingly is fundamental to good teaching, and a knowledge of how
the voice works is fundamental to good speaking.

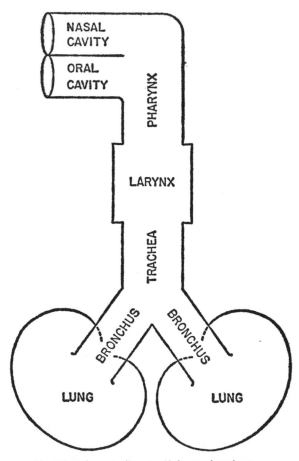

Fig. 1-1. Schematic diagram of the vocal mechanism.

The vocal mechanism

The vocal mechanism is a fascinating set of tubes, valves, and chambers none of which was really intended for the process of speech. There are the *lungs,* designed, of course, to serve us in the breathing process, bringing vital oxygen to the blood stream and thus sustaining life itself. There are the *bronchial tubes* and the *trachea,* whose primary purpose is simply to serve as an ever-open passageway by which air can move in and out of the lungs, to and from the world outside us. At the top of the trachea is the *larynx.* This is a sort of box made of several cartilages, which we often call the *Adam's Apple.* Inside it are the *vocal folds,* which act as deflectors when bits of food or liquid confuse the passageway to the lungs with the passageway to the stomach. Above the larynx is the *pharynx* or throat, which acts sometimes as an air scoop, and sometimes as a food funnel. Above the pharynx are the mouth and nose. Figure 1-1 is designed to show you these various parts, and their relationship to one another.

Somehow we have learned to use these various organs, passageways, and cavities of our bodies to produce meaningful sounds in sequence; but we should never lose sight of the basic fact that speech is, above all, an overlaid function. There is no part of the human body exclusively intended for the act of speech.

Breathing for speech

Speech takes place on the exhaled breath. This means, obviously, that breathing is basic to speech, and that exercises designed to improve and develop your breath control will probably help you have a better speaking voice. There has been a lot of nonsense written about this relationship, however, and it would probably be wise to stick to the facts.*

1. *It takes little or no more breath to speak than it takes to live.*

* For a good summary of the best knowledge available on the relationship between breathing and speech, see Charles Van Riper and John V. Irwin, *Voice and Articulation* (Englewood Cliffs, N. J.: Prentice-Hall, Inc., 1958), pp. 351-353.

Breathing exercises designed to increase your chest expansion may improve your physique and "tone up" your over-all reflexes, but they are largely irrelevant to your effectiveness as a speaker.

2. *Breathing centered in the lower trunk is not necessarily "the best" way to breathe for speech.* Good speakers seem to be good regardless of whether they have high chest breathing or diaphragmatic breathing. If your voice is weak, however, and sounds immature or colorless, it may be that it is not being properly "supported" by the breath, and that therefore the throat muscles are working overtime. Diaphragmatic breathing, then, *may* help you, and exercises designed to develop it *may* be of real value to you—but not necessarily!

3. *Breathing for speech is not essentially different from any other kind of breathing—except in terms of rhythm.* When you sleep the breathing cycle tends to be quite regular and even, with the inhalations and the exhalations being about equal in duration. But breathing for speech is characterized by a quick inhalation and a prolonged exhalation. The pattern in *vegetative breathing* is regular; in *speech* the pattern is irregular. In this one sense there **is** a difference, and exercises related to breathing rhythm can be of real value.

"VEGETATIVE BREATHING"

"BREATHING FOR SPEECH"

Fig. 1-2. The rhythm patterns of breathing.

Since breathing is basic to speech, let us consider the breathing process itself. First of all, we must think of the human body. That section encompassed by the rib cage we know as the *thorax*. Within

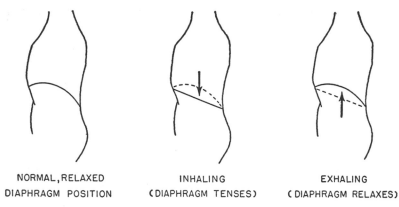

NORMAL,RELAXED INHALING EXHALING
DIAPHRAGM POSITION (DIAPHRAGM TENSES) (DIAPHRAGM RELAXES)

Fig. 1-3. The action of the diaphragm.

the thoracic cavity are the lungs. The floor of the thorax is principally formed by a large muscle called the *diaphragm*. When the diaphragm is relaxed it is somewhat dome shaped (see Figure 1-3). When it tenses, it flattens out and lowers. Tension in the diaphragm means, then, that the volume of the thorax will be increased because the floor of the whole cavity drops and flattens. At the same time the diaphragm is tensing, the muscles between the ribs (primarily the exterior intercostals) also tense, pulling the rib cage up and out. As a result of these two actions, the thoracic cavity is considerably increased in volume. Air pressure consequently causes air to come in through the mouth or nose, down through the pharynx, the larynx, the trachea, and the bronchi to the lungs. The lungs are made of numerous little sacs which fill with air, each one serviced by capillaries so that the body may absorb what it needs for life from the air itself and may dispose of its burnt fuel, carbon dioxide.

When the diaphragm and the muscles between the ribs relax, the abdominal muscles contract, forcing the inner visceral organs to push back into position, and helping the diaphragm to regain its dome-like shape again. Thus the chest volume is decreased, forcing air out of the spongy tissue of the lungs and back up through the same passageway by which it entered. Inhalation, then, is the result of *tensing* thoracic muscles. Exhalation is the result of *relaxing* these muscles, while simultaneously tensing certain of the abdominal muscles.

The principal muscle of breathing is the diaphragm. By its action it can, with the least expenditure of energy and effort, regulate the rate of breathing and the amount of intake and expulsion. It is a large, single muscle, capable of acting with greater ease than the complex system of muscles regulating the ribs. It is a simple principle of engineering that it is easier to change the volume of a pyramid by elevating or lowering its base than by changing the angle of its point. Since the chest area is roughly pyramid shaped, this principle would seem to apply.

Muscles operate in terms of what is called *agonism and antagonism*. Essentially, this means that as one muscle tenses it must pull against something—often another tensed muscle—in order to permit smooth, easy movement rather than spastic, jerky, uncontrolled movement. Because muscles work in this way, many singing teachers and teachers of speech counsel their pupils to use diaphragmatic breathing rather than high chest breathing. The muscles interacting in breathing centered in the high chest area might cause unneeded and unwanted throat tension, which could mean bad voice quality or vocal strain. The muscles interacting with the diaphragm, however, would be in the abdomen and across the back—far removed from the vocal folds themselves.

By breath control, then, we mean controlling the rhythm and capacity of the breathing itself. An effective speaker has breath enough for proper phrasing; exhalation even enough for a smoothly produced, well-modulated voice quality; and quiet enough, rapid enough inhalation to permit fluency and prevent gasping.

Little children with weak voices are often reacting with shyness to their notion of their environment. What may be needed from you as their teacher is assistance in the development of self-confidence and poise rather than breathing exercises. A sensible first step, however, would always be medical examination. If the family doctor or school nurse finds no organic reason for the faulty voice production, and your own best efforts to make the child more audible through ordinary methods of encouragement and good will are of no avail, special work with a trained clinician is called for. Serious vocal cases will not clear up without professional therapy.

As the child approaches adulthood there are definite physical changes which take place in the size and shape of the larynx. These changes often lead to serious, though temporary, vocal problems. Boys should be encouraged to use their lower tones as their voices change, and great care should be taken not to "push" their voices by prolonged drill; by too much loud, high or low singing; or by working for long periods with such vocally taxing materials as highly emotional declamations, orations, or dramatic scenes. Normal yelling and screaming will be enough of that sort of thing! Girls' voices change, too—although the change is primarily one of quality rather than of pitch. For them, as for boys, probably the best thing to do is to offer encouragement by explaining what is going on, and to be careful not to let them strain or misuse their changing voices. Some boys and girls will find that medial or diaphragmatic breathing habits are helpful when developed at this time—and moderation in all things vocal will be helpful to all.

Producing a sound

The vocal folds are housed in a box of cartilage called the *larynx,* the voice-box or Adam's Apple. The large cartilage which you can feel in the front is the *thyroid.* It is essentially butterfly-shaped. Inside it, and at the bottom, is a ring-shaped cartilage called the *cricoid,* which is about half again as big as your finger-ring. On top of the cricoid are perched two small pyramids of cartilage known as the *arytenoids.* The *vocal folds* are shaped like lips, attaching at the back to the arytenoids and in front to the thyroid, just below and behind the thyroid notch. The vocal folds anchor on the sides to various parts of the inner wall of the larynx, but mainly to the cricoid. The opening between them is called the *glottis.* Figure 1-4 shows these cartilages from the top, from the side, and from the front, and indicates their general structural relationship to one another.

As the air is forced up from the lungs, the vocal folds tense

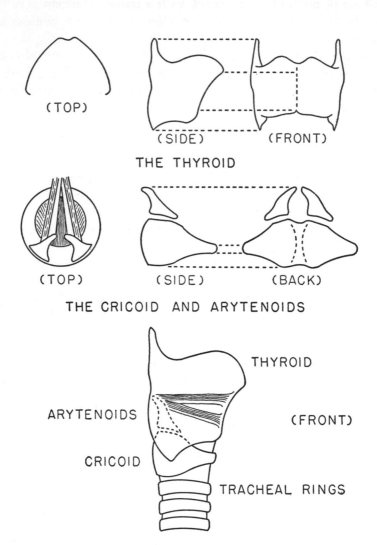

(TOP)

(SIDE)   (FRONT)

THE THYROID

(TOP)   (SIDE)   (BACK)

THE CRICOID AND ARYTENOIDS

THYROID

ARYTENOIDS   (FRONT)

CRICOID

TRACHEAL RINGS

THE LARYNX

Fig. 1-4. The cartilages of the larynx.

across the glottis in the larynx. When the air pressure in the trachea is great enough to overcome the tension in the vocal folds themselves, they are forced apart, letting a puff of air escape. Since the tension in the vocal folds remains fairly constant, this same process is repeated again and again. Thus we have in existence two possible sources of sound: vibrating lips and a vibrating column of air. It seems probable that both play a part in the phonation process, but experts generally agree upon the vocal cord vibration as the source of human sound.*

The sound produced in the larynx, however, is not yet the voice we hear. The cord-tone is weak, thin, and colorless. It has pitch, loudness, and duration, but little quality or timbre. As the sound passes through the pharynx, the mouth, and even—to some extent —the nose, it is amplified and modified through the process we call *resonation.*

Any sound is the result of the interpretation our ears give to a sound wave. There is an old riddle about whether or not there would be a sound if a tree fell in the forest with nobody around to hear it. The answer should be both yes *and* no. There would be a sound wave, but there would be no true "sound." A sound, in other words, has both physical and psychological aspects.

The sound wave itself is *movement* through something. Obviously, when I speak to you the little chunks of air next to my vocal cords do not fly through space and batter your eardrums! Instead, the rapid, synchronized, harmonic movement of the vocal folds in my throat creates a *condition of disturbance* which passes through space to your eardrums. These sensitive membranes vibrate in sympathy with the pattern of the wave vibration itself, setting off a chain of nervous reactions which the brain interprets as this or that sort of a sound. Even from this simple explanation, it is apparent that impairment of hearing or even deafness can stem from any one of several possible problems: some deficiency in the eardrums so they cannot vibrate with proper responsiveness;

* See James M. O'Niell *et al., Foundations of Speech* (Englewood Cliffs, N. J.: Prentice-Hall, Inc., 1942), pp. 125-126. This portion is written by Dr. William J. Temple. See also Wilmer T. Bartholomew, *Acoustics of Music* (Englewood Cliffs, N. J.: Prentice-Hall, Inc., 1942), pp. 140 ff.

some deficiency in the ability of the nervous system to transmit messages properly; some deficiency in the ability of the brain to translate the messages it receives. If you, or any of your pupils, experience hearing difficulty, again the first step is a medical examination. In many cases simply freeing the eardrums of inhibiting wax is of great help. In some cases hearing aids are called for, while in other cases very little can be done except to develop the child's skill in lip-reading. In all cases of serious hearing disability, expert guidance is needed.

If you find it difficult to understand how a condition of disturbance can pass through a medium such as air, stand a set of dominoes up on end in a line, placing them about half an inch apart. After they are all in line, tick the first one with your finger, knocking it into the next one. Then watch the condition of disturbance you have created pass through the whole line.

Imagine, if you will, that air, walls, trees, stones—all are made up of millions of tiny particles which have room enough to move slightly. As the vocal folds move the particles nearest them, these particles in turn push the next ones, which push the next ones, and so on. Each particle, therefore, bounces back and forth, setting up a motion rather like that of a pendulum. All particles will not be doing the same part of their "dance" at the same instant; thus we find that a sound wave has in it what we call *condensations* and *rarefactions*, occurring in alternation. The number of these created per second by the sound source is called the frequency of the sound wave. The distance from home base each particle moves in its excursion is called the amplitude of the wave. The regularity-irregularity of the pattern of condensations and rarefactions is called the wave composition. In Figure 1-5 a sound wave has been stopped, and the position of the various air particles is shown as if at a single instant. Some are moving out, some are moving back, some are just passing "home base," and others are perhaps at the end of their outward swing.

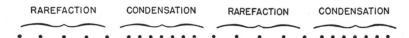

Fig. 1-5. The moving particles in a sound wave.

To simplify the understanding of a sound wave, scientists have thought up a way of drawing what a wave looks like. As the wave comes through air it is received by a large drumhead, setting it in sympathetic motion. The motion of the drumhead causes a pen to move back and forth across a never-ending roll of paper. When the drumhead moves out, the pen goes up; when the drumhead moves in, the pen goes down. In this way we get a picture of a sound wave which we can analyze. The mechanism is a relatively simple one, as Figure 1-6 shows.

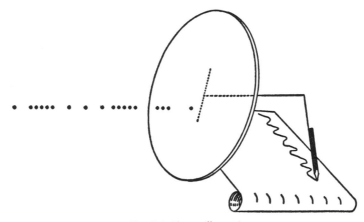

Fig. 1-6. The oscillograph.

When the over-all wave form moves in a regular pattern back and forth across the base line in the center of the paper, we have a picture of a tone. When the pattern has no regular shape, we have a picture of noise. The difference in contour between the two, as they would be drawn by the oscillograph, is shown in Figure 1-7. The number of times the base line is crossed in a second shows the frequency of the sound wave; the height-depth of the main contour of peaks and valleys above and below the base line shows the amplitude; the pattern itself shows the wave composition. When the ear receives any sound wave, it reacts with *sound,* translating the frequency as pitch, the amplitude as loudness, and the wave composition as quality.

In vocal tone, frequency and amplitude are the results of the

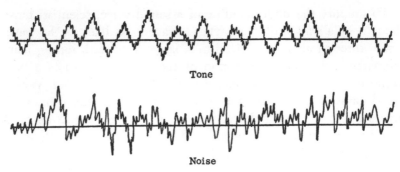

Tone

Noise

Fig. 1-7. Sound waves.

way we set the vocal folds in vibration. Every sound source has its own peculiar wave composition; thus the violin wave looks different from the wave made by the tympani or the harp. The human voice, however, mainly because of its flexible resonators, can produce many sorts of sound waves.

For example, shape your mouth to say *oo*. Now shape it to say *ee*, and now *ah*. Say these three sounds one after the other without a break, and without changing pitch or loudness. The vocal cords will vibrate the same way in all three sounds unless you change loudness or pitch, yet there is an obvious difference in the three sounds. The vowels, in other words, are not produced by the vocal cords, but are the result of resonance changes created by adjusting the shape and size of the mouth—the principal resonator of the human voice.

Analyzing and improving your voice

The following exercises are designed to help you do several things. Do not start at the first and sort of "work your way through," but begin instead by making some intelligent self-analysis. If at all possible, make a tape recording of your voice and listen to it objectively. Is it rich and full, or is it harsh, nasal, or breathy? Is it well-pitched, or does it seem to be unnecessarily high or low? Is your tone "supported," or does it seem weak and feeble? If you cannot make a tape, work with someone else in the class, perhaps criticising and evaluating one another. Your analysis need not be overly detailed in order to be helpful. Your purpose is to try to isolate a few things to work on—to make more specific that vague feeling which most of us have that our speech needs somehow to be improved. Consider your voice carefully, with the following things in mind: *pitch, loudness*, and *quality*. These things we have talked about already. In the next chapters we will talk about: *rate, articulation and pronunciation*, and *variety and expressiveness*. You may want to give these some thought now, as a part of your self-evaluation, even though you have not studied them specifically as yet.

Diaphragm action. The basis of good voice production is the way in which the breath is controlled and used. Can you control your breathing from the diaphragm? Whether or not you need to do so personally in order to have a good voice, try some of these exercises to see if you can do it.

1. Place the tips of the fingers of your left hand lightly against your abdomen above the belt line, and just below where your ribs and sternum join. Now pant like a dog. Can you move your fingers in and out by the natural movements of your breathing, or must you use conscious muscle action from the abdomen to move them? You should be able to feel a movement caused by your breathing alone if your diaphragm is at work.

2. Stand tall and straight, with your back against a wall, with heels, hips, shoulders, and head touching it. Have a partner take his book, and lean on it, pressing against your abdomen while you breathe. As you breathe in, if your diaphragm is at work, you will push against the book, actually moving your friend out and away from you!

3. Stand up, bend over as far as you can from the waist and relax. Let your head and arms dangle loosely. Once you are completely relaxed, without straightening up, put your hands on your waist with the thumbs to the front just under your lowest rib, and with the fingers reaching across the small of your back. Keep as relaxed as you can while you breathe deeply in and out several times. The diaphragm attaches along the lower ribs and to the spinal column. If your diaphragm is in control, you should feel

16 THE VOICE

expansion through the waist and across the back as you inhale. Now stand erect and see if you can reproduce this feeling as you breathe while standing naturally.

Diaphragm control. Now that you know what is meant by diaphragm action, the next question to ask yourself is whether or not you can put the diaphragm to work controlling the breath during the act of speech.

1. Place your hands on your abdomen just below the belt-line. Now cough. Do you feel the diaphragm spasm required for this action? Using the same inward-pulling that accompanies the cough, count out loud as if you were giving the cadence for a military drill—One—Two—Three—Four; One—Two—Three—Four. Take a quick breath before each number. As you do this exercise, be sure your throat does not tense. Also, have a partner check to be sure you keep your shoulders still. Your purpose is to support the tone you are producing—to inhale easily and quickly the breath you need to produce a loud tone, controlling this exhalation from the trunk of the body rather than from the throat.

2. Hold a small, lighted candle about 8 inches in front of your mouth. Say *ah* as long as you can, and watch the flame. Does it flicker, or go out? The flame, responding to the evenness and steadiness of your exhalation, should bend evenly away from you if your diaphragm is at work.

3. Using your hands as monitors, try a few school cheers, or military commands—anything. Is your diaphragm in control? If not, can you get it operating?

Relaxing the throat. Breathing, of course, is not the whole story. With the bellows in proper activity, however, we can next turn our attention to the vibrating sound source in the throat.

1. Yawn. Put your hand on your Adam's Apple. Now yawn again. Do you feel the larynx drop and the pharynx expand? This is the position the throat assumes when you correctly produce a big voice.

2. Pant again, only this time say *ha!* on each exhaled breath. Keep your throat open and relaxed. (You may need to stop and yawn a few times to check yourself.) The proper balance of tension

in the larynx against pressure from the breath stream should result in almost "sensationless" production of the tone. As you continue the exercise, clear the tone of breathiness, and quiet the inhalation until you are saying the syllable *ha* in a clear, easy, full voice.

Resonance. A good speaking voice requires not only good breath control and a relaxed throat, but also good resonance. The open throat adds to this resonance, of course, but a relaxed, open mouth is even more important.

1. Place two fingers of your left hand between your teeth, holding your mouth open two-fingers wide. Keep them there while you yawn. As the breath escapes after the yawn, sigh on an *ah*. Then try *oh* and *ee*. If your jaw is not relaxed, you will bite your fingers. Can you get this same open, free tone without the finger-props or the yawn?

2. Stand in front of a mirror and recite "Mary had a little lamb." Watch yourself. Is your jaw moving, or is it tight—rigid—stiff? Try to get your mouth open. If this big resonator is not used, the voice cannot be at its best. Drop your jaw, and rub your cheeks and jaw downward lightly with the palms of your hands until you relax. You may need to let your head sink forward on your chest, relaxing the muscles of your neck first. If you do, rotate your head slowly from side to side. With this relaxed feeling, recite to the mirror again. The mouth will probably open more, and the jaw will probably be less tense. The voice may sound a bit "moronic" because the relaxation is so complete, but with practice you can add life and color without adding tension.

3. Some voices have too much nasal resonance. Check yours by using a simple phrase which includes no *m*, *n*, or *ng* sounds. These three English sounds are supposed to be nasal. Hold your nose and say, "How are you today?" Now let go of your nose and say it. Does it sound and feel the same? It should. If it does not, try opening your mouth more, relaxing your throat more—anything—until the two phrases do sound and feel the same. Try to figure out what you did, and then try to make this new way of speaking a part of your daily life. It will not be easy to change the habit of a lifetime, so do not try to change all of your speech patterns at

once. Think of some phrase which you frequently use that has problem sounds in it which are likely to be nasal. Practice it carefully until you know that you can say it properly any time that you wish. Then set for yourself the task of using that phrase, properly resonated, three times each day. You will find that you will have fun with this game, and that soon you will be hearing other nasalized phrases, too, and correcting them. Ow (as in cow), ay (as in day), and the short a (as in cat) are trouble-makers for many people. Using the technique of holding the nose and then letting go, try the phrase: "The sow ate the hat." This can tell you whether you are having trouble with these sounds. Words with m, n, or ng in them are the worst offenders, of course, so check words like can, town, and rain, especially. Do not let nasal sounds mar your speech.

Your voice has a natural pitch level, which may or may not be the one you use habitually. Sing down as low as you can go—clear down to the very lowest tone you can hang onto, no matter how it sounds. Use that tone as one, and sing up the scale, counting as you go—one number to each note—all the way up to the highest squeak you can muster. This top tone will probably be between 12 and 24 somewhere, with 16 to 22 being about average. Take whatever your highest number was, divide it by four and round it off. Now go back to your lowest note again, and count your way up to this new number. This pitch is probably about where you should be talking. In other words, your natural pitch is probably about one-fourth of the way up your total pitch range. If you are habitually talking very much above or very much below this pitch, you should strive consciously and determinedly to change your vocal habits.

If your pitch level is naturally high (and for boys this can be especially serious), a pitch one or two notes below the natural pitch can usually be used with safety, unless you also use a tense throat. Find your natural pitch or one near it on the piano. Match this tone with your own voice and chant something. Then, as you talk along, use more and more pitch variation until you are talking naturally, with your speech pitch focused where it should be.

Summary

The basic vocal mechanism includes a source of energy (the *lungs*), a vibrating source (the *larynx*), and a resonator (principally the *pharynx,* and the oral and nasal cavities). Effective speech is based upon using this rather complex mechanism with good taste and with efficiency. Our voices have God-given limitations, but every voice is capable of effective usage. Speech is an aspect of human behavior. As such it can be changed; with suitable care, it can be changed for the better.

STUDY QUESTIONS

1. Without looking at Figure 1-1, can you diagram the seven major areas of the vocal mechanism?

2. Naming the bones and muscles involved, how do we breathe?

3. What is meant by the term, *breath control?*

4. In what sense is the diaphragm the principal muscle of breathing?

5. Without looking at Figure 1-4, can you diagram the larynx, showing the relative positions of the thyroid, cricoid and arytenoid cartilages?

6. How is a sound produced in the larynx?

7. What is the nature of a sound wave? What wave characteristic is evaluated by the ear as pitch? loudness? voice quality?

8. In what sense is the mouth the most important resonator so far as speech is concerned?

9. How can the *natural pitch* be determined?

10. A good speaking voice is free of nasality, harshness, hoarseness, and breathiness. How can this excellence of voice be best attained?

SUGGESTED CLASS ACTIVITIES

1. Prepare a short prose passage (not over 250 words) to read aloud. Try to think about reading *to* the others in the class. Consciously work to interest them, and to make the author's ideas clear. If at all possible,

your reading should be tape recorded so you can hear it yourself. After you have read, discuss your voice with others in your class and with your teacher. Try to discover where they think you might work for an even better voice, and compare their ideas with your own self-analysis. Then make a work sheet of drills designed to help you improve. (Drills can be found in the various books on voice and diction which are in your library.) When your work sheet is completed, let your teacher check it over and offer suggestions, then go to work.

2. Memorize Hamlet's "Advice to the Players," which follows:

Speak the speech, I pray you, as I pronounced it to you, trippingly on the tongue: but if you mouth it, as many of your players do, I had as lief the town-crier spoke my lines. Nor do not saw the air too much with your hand, thus; but use all gently: for in the very torrent, tempest, and, as I may say, whirlwind of passion, you must acquire and beget a temperance that may give it smoothness.

Practice the passage diligently, using the best-supported, freest, most fully resonant tone you can. Be prepared to declaim it from the stage of a large auditorium, or outdoors. Here you will encounter problems of *projection* which will tempt you to strain in order to be heard. Be sure, however, to resist—using the full breathing of diaphragm action, the relaxed throat and jaw, and the open mouth and pharynx. Do not worry if the pitch level seems a little high, for this naturally accompanies an increase in loudness. Try, however, to keep the pitch level as low as you comfortably can.

SUPPLEMENTARY MATERIALS

Akin, Johnnye, *And So We Speak*, Englewood Cliffs, N. J.: Prentice-Hall, Inc., 1958, Chapter 8, "Respiration for Speech," Chapter 9, "Phonation for Speech," and Chapter 10, "Resonation for Speech." A clear, up-to-date treatment of these aspects of the speech process.

Hahn, Elise, Charles W. Lomas, Donald E. Hargis, and Daniel Vandraegen, *Basic Voice Training for Speech*, New York: McGraw-Hill Book Co., 1957, Chapter 1, "Critical Listening and Self-Analysis," and Chapter 2, "Why You Speak as You Do." Helpful and suggestive chapters, well-written for the person who wants to work his own problems through.

Johnson, T. Earle, "Nasality in Southern Speech," *Southern Speech Journal*, Vol. XVII (September, 1951), pp. 30-39. Only the last few pages actually deal with "Southern" speech, while the rest is an excellent general summary of the literature on nasality.

Mulgrave, Dorothy, *Speech*, The College Outline Series, New York: Barnes & Noble, Inc., 1954, Chapter 11, "The Mechanisms of Speech and Hearing." A brief, yet detailed treatment; written clearly, in handbook style.

Sound Waves and Their Sources, and *Your Voice*, Encyclopaedia Britannica Films, 1150 Wilmette Ave., Wilmette, Illinois. Both are adult, clear, brief, and pertinent. Although they are somewhat dated, the datedness is not serious or objectionable.

2

Diction

It is true, of course, that a great many speech faults go unnoticed when the speaker is seemingly well-informed and is responsive to his own ideas and to his audience. If a person has something to say, and can say it in a sincere, earnest, lively way, we will readily forgive a slight nasality or breathiness of tone, or even an occasional mispronunciation. It should go without saying, however, that given a friendly sense of communication, good ideas, *and* good diction—all three—the speaker's chances of effectiveness are better than when he has enthusiasm alone.

In the previous chapter, "The Voice," we began making you aware of how you *sound* to others. In this chapter we are concerned with the modifications you make on that basic sound to shade it and adapt it to the needs of speech. An awareness of both concepts is necessary while learning to speak well.

The sounds of speech

Our words are generally said to be made up of two kinds of sounds: those which are *open-voiced* or produced without any particular obstruction or deviation of the breath stream, and those which are produced as a direct result of some stoppage or deviation of the breath stream. The first group of sounds we call vowels; the second we call consonants.

Vowel and consonant *sounds* are not to be confused with the vowels and consonants of spelling. In spelling, for example, the vowels are *a, e, i, o, u,* and sometimes *y;* but in speech, when we talk of vowels, we mean all of the sounds we make with the nasal cavity practically closed off and a vocalized breath stream passing freely through the opened mouth. We shape the mouth, round the lips, and tense and relax the tongue and jaw to change these vowel sounds and make them different from one another.

Whisper *ee,* and then without stopping whisper *ah.* Do you feel the change in the shape of your oral cavity? For *ee* the tongue rises, and the breath stream seems to strike the roof of the mouth toward the front. For *ah* the mouth is open and the breath stream seems to stay in the pharynx itself, rather than coming forward into the oral cavity proper. Each vowel sound has its own "shape," some with the breath stream striking in the front, and some with the breath stream staying back; some with the tongue and jaw fairly tense, and others with the tongue and jaw lax; some with the lips rounded, and some without.

If you will think where the breath stream seems to be aimed or focused as you say the various vowel sounds, Figure 2-1 will help you to understand the tongue positions which we typically use to produce them. The Table of Vowels arranges these sounds in another form, showing also which ones are lax or tense, rounded or unrounded.

In English, in addition to these common vowel sounds, we also regularly use three vowel combinations, or diphthongs. These are *ī* (as in *lie*), *ow* (as in *cow*), and *oy* (as in *boy*). If you will sing the word *I* for as long as you can hold it on one note, you will

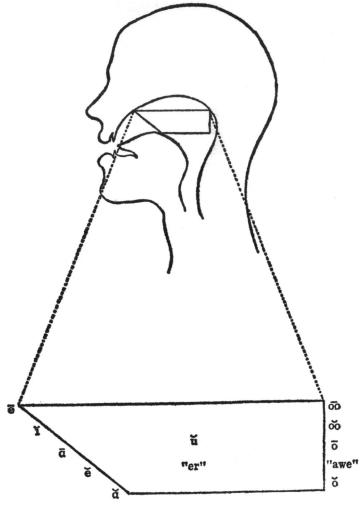

Fig. 2-1. Schematic diagram showing focus of the breathstream in production of the vowel sounds.

find that you actually seem to say *ah* . . . . *ee.* Similarly with *oy* (*awe* . . . . *ee*) and with *ow* (*ah* . . . . *o͝o*). In some cases our spelling for these three sounds even indicates this *double* characteristic, suggesting that a diphthong is actually

Table of Vowels*

Front vowels	Mid-vowels	Back vowels
ē as in *see*; high front, tense, unrounded	ŭ as in *hut*; mid central, lax, unrounded	ōō as in *boot*; high back, tense, rounded
ĭ as in *sit*; high front, lax, unrounded	"er" as in *heard*; mid central (retroflex) tense, half-rounded	ŏŏ as in *book*; high back, lax, rounded
ā as in *day*; mid front, tense, unrounded		ō as in *boat*; mid back, tense, rounded
ĕ as in *set*; mid front, lax, unrounded		"awe" as in *bought*; mid back, lax, rounded
ă as in *sat*; low front, lax, unrounded		ŏ as in *hot*; low back, lax, unrounded

* There seems to be no special reason to consider separately the unstressed "er," as in *mother*. Regional vowels, also, have been omitted.

a vowel combination, so rapidly and so frequently pronounced that it has come to be thought of as a single sound.

For example, although most *i* words simply use *i* in the spelling, we do have *die, lie, tie, pie,* and so on, which show the diphthong. The *ow* sound is always spelled with two letters, as in *hour, out, allow, cow,* or *house*; and the *oy* is also always spelled with two letters, as in *boy, joy, boil, soil, voice,* or *coin.*

Although we listed *ā* and *ō* as vowels, for most of us they, too, are actually diphthongs. Americans almost always add an *i* or an *ee* to their *ā* sound, and an *ōō* to their *ō*. These pronunciations are also recognized in spelling, as in *day, pay,* or *weigh*; and in *oak, oath, hoe, toe,* and *low.*

The commonest vowel or diphthong errors are: (1) the substitution of one sound for another, (2) the nasalization of the vowel or diphthong, and (3) the addition of other sounds to the simple vowel or diphthong. An example of the first sort of error occurs commonly in the confusion between *pen* and *pin*. It is also present in the fairly common mispronunciation of *fire* as *far*, or *poor* as *pore*. The most frequently nasalized sounds are likely to be *ā*, *ow*, *oy*, and *ī*, although others can also cause trouble. Examples of adding sounds include *bejud* for *bed*, *bawi* for *boy*, and *kaiou* for *cow*.

Despite the importance of such errors in enunciation, the clarity of our speech is much more dependent upon our consonants than it is upon our vowels and diphthongs. As a generalization, it is safe to say that the consonants make us *intelligible*, while the vowels give our speech its *pleasantness* of tone and its characteristic quality. After all, if a *t* is produced recognizably and audibly, it can scarcely be said to vary in its timbre from person to person in the sense that an *ā* or an *ō* will do so.

Some consonant sounds are non-continuant, while others (like vowels) may be sustained so long as there is breath. The non-continuant sounds are usually called *stop-plosives*, or *stops*, and are produced as their name suggests—by stopping the breath stream, and then exploding it suddenly. Examples are *p*, *b*, *t*, *d*, *k*, and hard *g*.

Continuant consonants are of several types, and their names also suggest their natures. Commonest are the *fricatives*, which are friction or noise sounds, including *f*, *v*, the hard and soft *th*, *s*, *z*, *sh*, *zh*, *h*, and *wh*. The three *nasals* are *m*, *n*, and *ng*. The *semivowels* are *l* and the consonant *r* (as in *tree* or *rain*). The *glides* are *w* and *y*.

Consonants are produced as a result of what we call *articulation*. In other words, certain movable portions of the mouth articulate with, or join together, or touch the fixed wall made up of the roof of the mouth, the teeth, and the gum ridge. These fixed areas, then, are not properly thought of as articulators. The lips and tongue, as well as the walls of the pharynx, the soft palate, and (in the case of *h*) even the vocal folds are the articulators, for they can move and articulate, whereas the hard palate, gums, and teeth cannot.

Many consonant sounds are like twins, in that they come in pairs of sounds, almost alike, except that one is spoken (voiced) and one is whispered (voiceless). Consider the two *th* sounds in "*this thistle.*" Obviously they are not alike—the *th* in *this* is voiced; the *th* in *thistle* is not. Other pairs include *p* and *b, t,* and *d, k,* and the hard *g, f,* and *v, s,* and *z,* and *sh* and *zh.* The Consonant Table will help you identify all these various consonant sounds according to their type, and their production.

Table of Consonants

	Nasals	Stop-plosives		Fricatives		Glides	Semi-vowels
		Voiced	*Voice-less*	*Voiced*	*Voice-less*		
Made with the lips (bilabial)	*m*	*b*	*p*		*wh*	*w*	
Lips and teeth (labio-dental)				*v*	*f*		
Tongue and teeth (lingua-dental)				hard *th*	soft *th*		
Tongue and gum ridge (post-dental, or lingua-alveolar)	*n*	*d*	*t*	*z* *zh*	*s* *sh*		*l* conso-nant *r*
Back of tongue and soft palate (velar)	*ng*	hard *g*	*k*			*y*	
Made in the glottis (glottal)					*h*		

The commonest consonant errors are: (1) the substitution of one sound for another, (2) interchanging the sounds of the voiced-voiceless pairs, (3) distorting or malforming the sound itself, (4) slighting or overemphasizing the sound, and (5) omitting, adding, or reversing sounds within a syllable or word.

Examples of substitution can be heard rather frequently in the speech of little children. The commonest adult substitutions are probably *th* for *s*, as in "Thith ith my thithter" (This is my sister); and the *w* for *l* and *r*, as in the classic phrase, "my wittow wed wagon" (my little red wagon). It is interesting that we tend to stereotype these substitutions as infantile. Less common clinically, although extremely common in daily speech is the substitution of *n* for *ng*, as in *nothin'*, *goin'*, *fishin'*, to which little or no value judgment of any kind is attached except that of sloppiness. The velar *ng* sound is harder to make than the post-dental *n*, which may account for its being so generally preferred. In urban speech we sometimes hear *d* for *th*, as in *dese* (these), *dem* (them), and *dose* (those).

Examples of voicing errors are also especially common in urban speech, where we hear *d* for *t* in *little*, *bottle*, and similar words, and a quite general use of *s* for *z* at the ends of words—as in "*boyss* and *girlss*."

The commonest distortions are those of the *s* sound, which is all too often either hissing or lateral. The hissing *s* (sometimes it even whistles!) needs to be tamed down so that less pressure is put behind it. Occasionally it needs to be produced in some new and different way, so the breath stream will not cut across the teeth in "just that one spot" which causes the extra sibilance, but usually the problem is pressure. The lateral *s* is produced softly, with the air stream coming out the sides of the mouth broadly rather than being focused sharply in the center. Although it is not really a *sh* sound, it moves in this direction. Neither of these *s* deviations is a true substitution, but they are, instead, errors in production.

Overemphasis of consonants is characteristic of the Bronx and Brooklyn dialects especially, although it tends to be a part of a great deal of urban speech everywhere. Interestingly enough, slighting of consonants is also characteristic of urban speech. Normal running speech requires a certain amount of slighting, of course, but—as with anything, even if it is good—too much is too much. For example, one should slight one of the *t* sounds in "Daisies don't tell," but "Whyntcha come overtuh night?" is inexcusable. The difficulty is to determine the difference between good diction and affected speech.

Common examples of omitting, adding, and reversing sounds are such pronunciations as *li-berry* for *library*; *drownded* for *drowned*, or *sta-stistics* for *statistics*; and *irrevelent* for *irrelevent*.

These, then, are the sounds of our speech: vowels, diphthongs, and consonants. Knowing how they are produced can help you check your own production. Learning to hear the various sounds in words will sharpen your whole awareness of diction and help you to improve your own clarity of speech. But even more important is the fact that this knowledge can help you help your students. If one of your third graders has some *s* problems, for example, you can help him with simple mirror drills to learn to keep his tongue back—to make an *s* and not a *th*. Similarly, you can teach the whisper-sound *t* instead of the spoken sound *d*, and so on. Basic understanding of the underlying principles of diction, plus some creative ingenuity can result in better teaching and better speech for you and for your pupils.

Remember, however, that many articulatory errors common to children in pre-school, kindergarten, and first grade seem to "just disappear" as more maturity develops. At this age, you should work toward nothing more than intelligibility, and do this only provided that you are careful not to set standards too high, not to nag too much, and not to make the children tense. After the second grade, however, if an articulatory problem persists despite your efforts, by all means seek professional help for your students. Articulatory problems sometimes have deep-seated physical and psychological causes rather than simply surface-level behavioral causes. When they do, it is wise to be working with trained assistance.

Influences upon your diction

When we talk about the pronunciation of words, we need, first of all, to understand that there is no *one* way to pronounce anything. The standard dictionaries offer good guidance, but pronunciations change—sometimes faster than editors can keep up. There is often an honest choice, in which cases the dictionary simply lists all possibilities and leaves it up to you.

In America we speak three principal versions of the English language. If you grew up in one of the states of the old Confederacy, or in a border area near the South, you probably have at least some traces of a Southern accent. If you grew up east of the Hudson, or in its valley, you may have Eastern speech—although Eastern speech is less certain to result in the East than is Southern speech in the South, for some sociological reason. If you grew up anywhere else in the United States, your speech is probably what we call General American. Figure 2-2 gives you the general outlines of these three big American dialect areas.

McBurney and Wrage, *The Art of Good Speech* (Prentice-Hall, Inc., 1953), p. 436.

Fig. 2-2. American dialect regions.

Within each of these areas there are real differences, of course. The dark *awe* sound which the person from Pittsburgh uses when he says *Bobby,* or *bought* is not at all native to the drawling speech of the man from Lubbock or Abilene, Texas. The *poosh, cooshion,* and *boosh* (for *push, cushion,* and *bush*) of the person from southern Indiana, southern Ohio, or West Virginia is foreign to the man from Emporia, Sacramento, or Boise. On the other hand, from Syracuse and Philadelphia to El Paso, Los Angeles, and Seattle, people talk more alike than different. Similarly, the speech of the girl from Mississippi is not like that of girls from North Carolina or Kentucky, yet their speech will be more alike than the speech of any of them will be like the speech of girls from Wyoming or the Dakotas.

It is interesting to notice, also, the urban and rural influences upon speech. Many people from New Orleans and many people from Detroit, Chicago, and New York have observable similarities of inflection and dialect. Some cities do not seem to be "urban" enough to have this influence upon their citizens, although their size would suggest urban speech as a possible pattern of development, while other cities that are relatively small—Mobile, for example—do seem to encourage some urbanisms. Characteristic of urban speech is a nasalization of certain vowels and diphthongs such as *ă* and *ow*, the use of an unvoiced *z* (*s*) at the ends of words, and the stressing of consonants, giving the over-all speech a clipped, punched, nasal, driving kind of delivery. Rural speech tends to equalize emphasis on all syllables, to slight consonants without running words together, and to nasalize.

In other words, the dialect region will affect acceptable pronunciation patterns, as will—in some cases—the rural or urban character of the area. In addition, such influences as geographic and social isolation play their role in the development of the speech of such groups as the Ozark or Appalachian mountaineers, the Pennsylvania Dutch, or the Southern Negroes. Good speech can be regional, of course, but radio, television, and the motion picture are all breaking down the linguistic barriers between dialect groups. General American speech is the prevailing standard, and even good Southern or Eastern speech will call attention to itself outside those regions. Ruralisms and urbanisms alike are likely to be substandard, and should probably be eradicated, or at least soft-pedaled. Your guide should be the best speaking of the best speakers of your community, and the general pattern of radio and television performers—especially the announcers. In the case of individual words, of course, the dictionary is a helpful general aid.

Analyzing and improving your diction

If you do not want the children in your class to develop substandard speech, you cannot permit yourself to have it. Tape record
a conversation between yourself and someone else, then play it
back and analyze it. Are you running too many words together?
Are you easy to understand?

The following exercises are designed to help you avoid the
common vowel and diphthong errors. Before beginning them, the
exercises in Chapter 1 which deal with nasality should be used
again. Check carefully your *ā, ă, ow, oy,* and *ī* sounds. Remember,
too much nasal resonance can mar otherwise excellent speech.

1. Consider next the matter of vowel substitution. The commonest is probably the use of *ī* for *ĕ*. Work on these pairs of words
to be sure you make a difference between them:

pin-pen	kin-ken	tin-ten	him-hem
sit-set	big-beg	Min-men	Minnie-many

When you are sure that you are hearing and making the difference,
try these words. The italicized letters should all be pronounced
as *ĕ*.

get	*e*ngineer
ag*a*in	chemistry
*a*ny	T*e*nnessee

The following words, on the other hand, should all be said with *ī*:

king	ring
sing	rinse
think	since
drink	milk

2. Now go over the words in these last two lists deliberately
using the wrong sounds. Say *git*, following it with *get; agin, again;
inny, any,* and so on. In the second list, say *keng, king; seng, sing;*
and so on. Can you hear and make the differences?

3. Check the following words, also. They are frequently mis-
pronounced in rural speech.

pronunciation *not* pro-noun-ciation
fire *not* far
tire *not* tar
poor *not* pore *or* purr
put *not* putt
egg, leg, keg *not* aig, laig, kaig
unable, unlikely, unnecessary *not* on-able, on-likely, on-necessary
can *not* kin
can't *not* kaint
for *not* fur
catch *not* ketch
just *not* jist
sofa, soda *not* sofy, sody
our *not* are

4. Check yourself on these words to be sure that you are not adding any syllables or sounds:

film *not* fillum
elm *not* ellum
frailty *not* frail-i-ty
cruelty *not* cru-lity
athlete, athletic *not* ath-uh-lete, ath-uh-letic
grievous *not* griev-i-ous
mischievous *not* mis-chiev-i-ous
brethren *not* breth-uh-run

5. Be sure no *r* sound is added at the end of such words as:

law   idea
saw   Claudia

6. The following sentences have problem vowels and diphthongs to which there is a temptation to add other sounds. Be sure that you can say them with clear, pure, open-voiced sounds, and that they do not become spread or flattened out into distorted syllables.

How now, brown cow, browsing loudly in the mow?
Sam sat in the class and waited for the man to stand.
Ben sent a hen.
The guide tried to get us to walk the mile-wide isle.

The following exercises are designed to help you avoid the common consonant errors.

1. Practice some tongue twisters. Good examples of these "limbering up" exercises are such "old chestnuts" as:

rubber baby-buggy bumper
Round and round the rugged rock the ragged rascal ran.
Peter Piper picked a peck of pickled peppers.
She sells sea-shells down by the seashore.

2. Work on lists of words with hard sound combinations such as:

stuffs	guests	lisps	tasks
puffs	lists	gasps	asks
coughs	beasts	wasps	disks
roughs	masts	rasps	tusks
sixth	watched	sneaked	smoothed
breadth	lunched	balked	bathed
strength	hatched	perked	breathed
length	lurched	tucked	wreathed
changed	washed	moved	saves
obliged	brushed	proved	loves
bridged	swished	paved	lives
hedged	flushed	dived	leaves

3. Paired words such as the following can help you check the clarity with which you produce that "little bit of difference" that makes good, clear speech:

whirled-world	sheath-sheathe
whether-weather	teeth-teethe
which-witch	wreath-wreathe
where-wear	ether-either
whale-wail	loath-loathe
wed-red	wet-let
wake-rake	weed-lead
won-run	wait-late
weed-read	wake-lake
wide-ride	wean-lean

4. Watch the problem *ng* at the ends of words. The careless substitution of *n* in its place is especially common in the following seven words:

nothing *not* nuthin'
doing *not* doin'
fishing *not* fishin'
going *not* goin'
coming *not* comin'
walking *not* walkin'
talking *not* talkin'

It is easy to make such lists of your own for various sound problems. Their purpose is not so much to train the tongue, however, as to train the ear. Most of our articulatory problems occur because we do not listen to ourselves when we talk. Drilling of this sort awakens us to what our tongue and lips must actually do to make a given sound clearly. At the same time it sharpens our consciousness of the sounds in words.

Summary

The sounds of speech are vowels, diphthongs, and consonants. Each is the result of a learned pattern of behavior: shaping the big resonator that is the mouth for the vowels and diphthongs and causing special obstructions and deviations in the breath-stream for the consonants. The key to good diction is necessarily accuracy of sound production, and only ear-training can bring this accuracy about. If there is no physical handicap and no mental deficiency or psychological block, bad diction is probably behavioral in its basis and therefore clearly removable. Regardless of sociological and geographic influences, good speech can be the result of careful listening when coupled with careful, accurate production of the various sounds.

STUDY QUESTIONS

1. Distinguish between the ways vowels and consonants are formed.
2. Define *diphthong*, and name the five which are common in American English.

3. Give examples of front vowels, mid-vowels, and back vowels. What do these terms mean?

4. What are the three commonest vowel and diphthong errors? Give an example or two of each.

5. Name and locate the articulators, and the hard, immovable walls against which they operate.

6. Define the terms *stop-plosive, fricative, nasal, semi-vowel,* and *glide.* Give an example of each of the kinds of sounds these terms describe.

7. Explain the difference between a voiced and a voiceless sound. Give three examples of voiced-voiceless pairs of consonant sounds.

8. What are the five commonest consonant errors? Give an example or two of each.

9. What are the three big American dialect regions?

10. Is there such a thing as one and only one correct pronunciation for a word?

SUGGESTED CLASS ACTIVITIES

1. Choose any poem which you like, and practice reading it aloud until you believe that all the words are intelligible. Read it to the class, asking your listeners to note down all unclearly said words. Compare the lists for agreement, and talk them over together. You might like to do this with a tape recorder if there is time to play your selection back. Excellent selections for this purpose are Poe's "The Bells," Robert Southey's "The Cataract of Lodore," Tennyson's "The Bugle Song," and Vachel Lindsay's "The Congo." Lewis Carroll's "Jabberwocky" offers an interesting challenge, too, as do the lyrics of almost any of the comic songs in the Gilbert and Sullivan operettas.

2. From your daily newspaper, select two or three items and write them up as if for a radio newscast. Read them to the class in a rapid, clear, energetic manner. Be sure to articulate clearly.

SUPPLEMENTARY MATERIALS

Fairbanks, Grant, *Voice and Articulation Drillbook,* New York: Harper & Brothers, 1940, "Sentences for Articulation Examination: Adult Readers," in the "Introduction." This is an excellent list of loaded sentences designed to put to the tongue every problem conceivable. Also interesting and useful are Chapter II, "Vowel Articulation," Chapter III, "Diphthong Articulation," Chapter IV, "Consonant Articulation," and Chapter V, "Pronunciation." All are filled with drill materials, and characterized by concise, specific explanations.

Van Riper, Charles, and John V. Irwin, *Voice and Articulation*, Englewood Cliffs, N. J.: Prentice-Hall, Inc., 1958, Chapter 1, "Abnormal Articulation," and Chapter 2, "The Causes of Defective Articulation." These are both highly authoritative chapters, reasonably readable, although detailed. Seemingly no piece of research on the subject has gone unstudied.

3

Expressiveness

We have already seen that the way we speak is subject to many influences, some from our inherited physical characteristics, and others from our family surroundings and our general cultural environment. With the exception of severe physical and psychological handicaps, most of the adverse influences upon our speech are either sociological or behavioral. As such they are learned, either as a part of our technique of adjustment to life, or as a part of our developing habit structure.

The job of bringing about a change in speech behavior is a complex one, sometimes rather difficult to accomplish. In one sense, however, it is not so complicated as it might seem, because there are only four basic variables in speech: pitch, loudness, rate, and quality. To these, of course, we add the complex functions of articulation and pronunciation, but all that can be done with the human voice is basically the result of the interaction of some or all of these factors. Instead of defining expressiveness at the outset, let us consider first the elements which produce it, and then attempt some over-all analysis.

Use of pitch

Natural and habitual pitch were explained in Chapter 1. It is possible to have a well-pitched voice, however, and still not be expressive. As we speak, the voice "sings" a melody. Technically we call this over-all process *intonation*. The individual shadings of melody which make up the intonation of a person or a language are called *inflection patterns*.

The intonation of each language is different. You have only to think of the stereotypes to know this to be true. How would you imitate Chinese, for example? or French? You have probably heard Mel Blanc imitate "Pedro," with his curiously rising inflection on "I theenk," and you may even be able to imitate the stock Swedish or Norwegian comic phrase, "Yumpin' Yimminy!" Although we are so used to it that we do not hear it, American English has its unique intonation, too.

The problem with American intonation is that the individual inflection patterns which make it up are likely to become monotonous. Sentences ending with periods usually have falling patterns, while questions almost always rise. Unless we watch, the contantly repeating falling inflection which characterizes our language can become deadly dull. Recite "Mary had a little lamb" all the way through rather rapidly, with no particular effort at expression, and you will see immediately what the problem is.

Equally as obnoxious as an improper pitch pattern is vocal monotony. Often a person who has a weak, breathy voice will complicate an already serious problem by failing to use vocal variety. Listen to people whom you consider to have good speech, on the other hand, and you will find, almost without exception, that they use a rather wide vocal range, and use it with variety.

Naturally, one does not develop variety that is effective just by "changing his tune." The person whose speech is dull because of pitch patterns or the person who has a monotonous voice has probably either failed to grasp the real meaning of what he is trying to say, or has not (for one reason or another) permitted himself to become involved or enthusiastic.

Pitch usage is clearly related to meaning and to emotion. In sadness, contempt, or indifference, for example, the pitch level is likely to be low, while in fear or anger it is likely to be high. Listen to the people around you, and you will quickly agree that the key to good pitch usage is a conscious awareness of what it is that one really wishes to say, and a genuine feeling of earnestness about saying it.

Use of loudness

Just as the pitch of a voice can be habitually too high or too low, a voice can also be habitually too loud or too soft. Similarly there are loudness patterns and a monotony of loudness. Probably the biggest problem so far as loudness is concerned, however, is simply the problem of being heard. Most student teachers have to learn that it takes more voice than they think it does to be heard easily in a classroom! This little matter of loudness probably comes in for more frequent adverse comment from practice teaching supervisors than does any other single point concerning the speech of student teachers. Good advice is to talk always to the people in the back row, and, moreover, to talk as if you *had* to make them listen.

Use of rate

We speak at a somewhat slower rate than we read aloud. The usual explanation for this is that when we speak we need more time for pauses, more time to think on our feet than when we read an author's already-thought-out words. Experts agree that our *normal* reading rate is about 135-170 words per minute, give or take ten, depending upon which expert you prefer.* The recorded speeches of Franklin Delano Roosevelt are definitely at the slow

---

* This is a compromise figure. Franke's 1939 study, cited in Grant Fairbanks, *Voice and Articulation Drillbook* (New York: Harper & Brothers, 1940), pp. 141-146, still seems authoritative.

end of this range, some of them even slower than 135 words per minute. On the other hand, Walter Winchell has been clocked at over 210!

As with pitch, however, the problem of ineffective use of rate is not so much one of some absolute level or standard as it is of variety. Some kinds of statements must be made slowly, while others can be speeded up effectively. In speech there is rhythm, and we need to be aware of it. The problem is to use it rather than to be used by it!

Recite the first lines of Longfellow's "Paul Revere's Ride," for instance, and you will find it almost impossible to keep from galloping off with Paul's horse!

> "Listen, my children, and you shall hear
> of the midnight ride of Paul Revere. . . ."

The basic beat is "dum-de-de-dum-de-de-dum-de-dum," and the hoofbeats are well-nigh inescapable. Here the poet is using rhythm for an obvious reason—as does Poe in "Bells," and Vachel Lindsay in "The Congo." In our everyday speech, however, repeated rhythmic patterns are undesirable.

One of the commonest objectionable patterns is the one in which every syllable is given the same stress regardless of what the words involved may be. Another is the extremely rapid, jerky rhythm which results in frequent omissions and distortions of sounds. Use your ears, and see if you can find people around you who speak too rapidly, and when you do, note the rushed, irregular rhythm of their speech. It sounds nervous, tense, even as if they were personally insecure. By all means, avoid this pattern in the classroom. It can go a long way to discourage in your students that calm feeling of acceptance for you which is basic to their learning. If your speech makes them empathize tension or nervousness, your classroom will not be for them a comfortable place. Perhaps you will find someone who speaks too slowly. Such people sound dull, listless, nerveless. Avoid this, also, because it will be boring. Genuine animation and enthusiasm are partly reflected in rate, just as they are partly reflected in pitch usage.

Use of quality

Good voice quality is sometimes defined as being the absence of such irritating characteristics as nasality, harshness, hoarseness, or breathiness. This oversimplifies things, however, because there are times when we want to use one or another of these kinds of voice quality to help us put across an idea or a mood more effectively. Perhaps you have heard recordings of some of Sir Winston Churchill's World War II speeches. The way in which he turned the word, Nazi, into a nasal snarl was an excellent means of putting across his feelings unmistakably, as well as a way of building certain feelings in his listeners. In other words, we sometimes deliberately use *bad* vocal quality in order to be more expressive.

As a rule, however, we strive for good rather than bad voice quality, and the ideas and exercises in Chapter 1 offer a helpful general guide.

Analyzing and improving your expressiveness

It is important to note that your voice and diction can be improved by careful, thoughtful analysis and drill, but your basic ability to be expressive probably cannot. Your expressiveness is integral with your responsiveness! They are two parts of the same whole. No amount of drill will ever make you expressive unless you are capable of responding to the feelings and ideas of others. Speech, after all, is essentially interpersonal. Even though we sometimes hear the phrase, "giving a speech," an effective person does not ever really "give a speech"; instead, he "speaks *to*" someone.

One of the best ways to teach children to be expressive is to teach them first to be responsive. The device of "sharing time" is excellent with the pre-schooler or the child in the early primary grades, because it provides a time when he can "give" of himself to others of the wonders he has come to know. With little children, expressiveness of speech is usually natural—especially if speaking is encouraged and permitted in a free and friendly atmosphere.

As we grow older, however, we forget to respond. Our lives

are busy and our thoughts tend to focus upon certain tasks to the exclusion of all others, until we lose the child's thrill of expression. Our voices become dull; our sentences without emphasis; our speech without interest to others because we have forgotten our obligation to be of interest to them.

The following exercises are designed to help you develop expressiveness in the sense that they will require you to think of communicating something in a context, to a person or group. Expressiveness does not have a chance when we are not aware of the whole act of communication, as it is seen in Figure 3-1. This

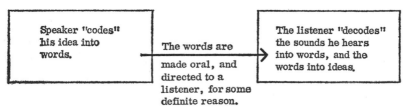

Fig. 3-1. A diagram of the act of communication.

act takes place within some context which not only motivates it but also affects it in many other ways. It is not a one-way process, but involves "feed-back," too. In other words, I do not speak to you until I see the two of us in a frame of reference where speech is possible. We could stand jammed together in an elevator and say nothing. When circumstances suggest communication, however, I put my idea into words and project them toward you, usually watching you in the hope of sensing your attentiveness, your interest, your comprehension. You will, as a rule, also watch me as I speak—at least you probably will once you are aware that I am addressing you. Thus, we have an essentially circular situation in which we are interacting by speaking and listening within a defined frame of reference. Our perceptors are our eyes and ears.

What, then, is expressiveness? Essentially it consists of anything I may do as a speaker to increase our mutual interaction. In one sense, we can describe expressiveness with such terms as sincerity, earnestness, enthusiasm, friendliness, and so on. In another sense we must use such terms as inspiring, moving, irritating, annoying, humorous, charming, and so on. At the operational level, it seems to mean our ability to make others feel what we want them to feel, and understand what we want them to understand.

1. A frequently used exercise is to take the word, *no*, and say it so that it means various things. Say it three or four times, if you like. This may help you get your idea across. As a start, see if you can say the word so that your listener will know that you mean:

absolutely not!
Oh, surely that can't be true!
Did you say, "no"?
Oh, I guess not after all.

2. Take a paragraph from the newspaper concerning some issue of state, local, national, or international government. Read it aloud as if you were highly indignant about what it says. Now read it again as if it pleased you thoroughly. What have you done to put these two moods across? How have you made the difference? Was it an adjustment in your use of pitch? loudness? rate? quality? several of these together?

3. Consider the sentence, "You want to go to town." How many different ways can you say it? What does it mean in each case?

In order to do these things you are using changes in the basic four factors of vocal delivery, and you are using these factors in definable ways. Certainly you are using what might be called *stress*, by which we mean any emphasis or prominence given any sound, syllable, word, or phrase for any purpose whatever. In diction, stress helps us to accent properly the syllables of words. In expressiveness, we use stress for both logical and psychological reasons: to make clear, and to make compelling or interesting.

Stress can be given by increasing loudness, by slowing rate, by the use of an anticipatory pause just before an important word or idea, by raising the pitch, by suddenly speaking more softly, by using a contrasting quality, and so on. In a sense we might define the whole of expressiveness as *stressing* certain ideas and images and moods by our delivery in order to make what we say more clear or more compelling to someone else.

As your own responsiveness becomes greater, you will find that others around you tend to become more responsive also. Make a mental note right now to encourage your pupils to learn to see and respond to the world about them vividly; to teach them the relationships of their moods and their voices; and to build into your classroom a sense of happy, wholesome interaction. You cannot do these things if your own speech is dull or monotonous. *You* will set the tone for everyone.

Summary

Your expressiveness is a reflection of your own interest in your message and your listener. It is basically a matter of *stress*, which you use in order to share more completely with your listener what you have to say. Your four tools are pitch, loudness, rate, and quality. Effective use of them requires, first of all, that you listen to yourself and to others, in order that you may be responsive in a vital and intelligent way. As Chesterton once sagely observed, "He who would shine must first light the lamp."

STUDY QUESTIONS

1. What are the four basic variables in speech?
2. What is intonation? Inflection?
3. What is probably the main intonation problem for speakers of American English?
4. What are the principal loudness errors?
5. What is the usual, or normal rate of speech in ordinary connected discourse? How does this rate differ from our "normal reading rate"?
6. What are two common rhythm problems in ordinary speech?
7. Can "bad" quality be useful under certain circumstances?
8. Define stress. Give several ways in which we can achieve stress in our speech.
9. Why does this chapter include so few exercises? Is it a fair generalization to assume that expressiveness can result from drill alone?
10. Explain the act of communication.

SUGGESTED CLASS ACTIVITIES

1. Divide the class into small groups and have them plan skits which will require expressiveness in order to put across characterization, mood, story, and so on. Use simple, well-known stories that will require little preparation. A good example is the story of "Little Red Riding Hood," or the episode of the homecoming of "The Three Bears." Corn it up as much as you can—remember that you cannot define the middle of a thing until you know its extremes! This exercise, of course, should not be graded. Its whole purpose is to get you to use variety of pitch, loudness, rate, and quality consciously and deliberately, for a real purpose rather than as a matter of drill. More serious kinds of episodes can be prepared, if you prefer, such as introducing a new teacher to certain people at a P.T.A. tea; having a conference with "irate parents," and so on.

2. Take turns relating a simple experience, using numbers instead of words. You will have your voice, and your gestures to help you tell your story, but not the usual meaning-bearing symbols we call words. See how much you can get across to your classmates.

SUPPLEMENTARY MATERIALS

Black, John W., and Wilbur E. Moore, *Speech: Code, Meaning, and Communication,* New York: McGraw-Hill Book Company, Inc., 1955, Chapter 12, "Interpretative Speech." A clear, learned study of the practical problems of speaking expressively. A key sentence is found on p. 261, "Too often the limitations of experience, both actual and symbolic, are barriers to the communication of experience."

Crocker, Lionel, *Interpretative Speech,* Englewood Cliffs, N. J.: Prentice-Hall, Inc., 1954, Lesson 9, "Mood, Atmosphere, Attitude." A brief, readable comment, filled with excellent materials for practice.

4

Posture and gestures

Writers of public speaking texts have been saying much the same things about the bodily action of speakers for several hundred years. For the most part they take one or the other of two positions. One set of suggestions can be summed up in the phrase, "Be natural," while the other set suggests a multiplicity of special rules and standards.

There is, of course, much to be said for either position. Gestures should indeed "arise naturally from within" in response to the speaker's wish to be understood and to be interesting. Unfortunately, however, some people are just naturally sloppy, others are just naturally stiff and unmoving. For such people the advice to be natural is relatively pointless. In fact, many amateurs find, when they "feel something within" that seems to call for a gesture, that the result is all too often a sort of half-hearted, embryonic wiggle of the hand instead of a controlled, compelling, full-fledged movement. Most people need more specific guidance than just the advice, "Relax and be yourself."

On the other hand, to move over into a completely mechanical approach such as the elocutionists of the "Mechanistic School" once used is probably not wise either. The James-Lange theory has shown us that we sometimes run because we are afraid, and at other times we are afraid because we are running. Applied to speech, this theory suggests that gestures can be superimposed upon the speaker's ideas, and that he will feel "effective" because he looks and acts the role of an effective speaker. It is true, of course, that William Jennings Bryan and many others of his day learned the art of gesture and applied it in this way. It is also true that many of the men and women taught by this method were able orators. For every William Jennings Bryan, however, there is at least a baker's dozen or more whose speaking never became anything other than affected, arty, and insincere. Most speakers who use the mechanical approach—sprinkling gestures here and there, taking a step deliberately at this point or that, and so on— end up with an artistic production in which all the art is showing. When art *shows*, it is bad. The listener should never see a gesture as a gesture. He should be aware only of the man speaking, and his ideas. Similarly, the speaker should never think of gestures as such while he is speaking. Such conscious affectation is even more to be avoided than most because it is so easy to spot. In our day the prevailing mode is not one of studied elegance, but of earnest conversation.

The posture of the good speaker

Consider for a moment how "the good speaker" stands or sits while he is talking. As a teacher you will be judged repeatedly as a speaker—for in many cases, as we have said, to teach *is* to talk. Your students will react to and talk about your mannerisms—just as you do with regard to the mannerisms of teachers you have. When you ask students to tell some experience during "telling time," to make a report on some aspect of their reading, or to share some observations growing out of a field trip or a film, what will you expect of them? There is more to it than just saying, "Stand up, Johnny." *How* do you want him to stand?

First of all, we should realize that no one talks from one and only one posture or position. Sometimes you will be standing at the board, at other times by your desk, or near the bulletin board or sand table. Sometimes you will be seated at your desk, or in a chair with the students gathered around you. How you stand and how you sit will communicate to your listeners, just as what you say communicates to them. What you primarily want your posture to say is, "I am interested in this and in you." You certainly do not want your posture to say, "This is dull," or "I can hardly wait to get this over with."

Consider the way you hand something to a person. To demonstrate it to yourself, assume that you are talking to a friend. Pick up a book or a pencil—whatever is near you—and pretend to hand it to him right now. What did you do? Did you lean *toward* him, or away from him? Now pretend that what you have been asked to hand over is a filthy, stinking pair of old tennis shoes. What do you do? Do you still lean in—or do you now lean away? When you are standing to speak and rock back on one heel, leaning away from your listeners, you are subliminally suggesting to them a lack of genuine, friendly interest—perhaps even suggesting dislike or distaste for them and for your topic, just as you suggested dislike or distaste for the dirty sneakers. In other words, the first rule for good posture is to interact with your listener in a way that is *toward* rather than *away from* him and his learning problems. This interaction will affect your posture, whether you are seated or standing.

A second thing to remember is that the eye follows lines. Artists have known this simple fact for centuries. Notice in Figure 4-1 how Leonardo da Vinci has used the lines of arms, the direction of eyes to focus the viewer's attention upon Christ in his masterpiece, "The Last Supper." Similarly, as you speak you present a picture to your listener. If you hide your hands behind your back, your listener's eyes will be pulled irresistibly down the lines of

Fig. 4-1. The use of lines for focus in "The Last Supper."

your arms and away from your face. He will be distracted by your stance. As a general rule, a good base posture has the hands hanging easily at the sides, or resting easily on a speaker's stand, the back of a chair, or the top of a desk. When you are seated, do not fold your arms, but rest them easily in your lap. In this way, as is shown in Figure 4-2, when the listener's eyes follow the lines of your arms they will be led back again to your face, not down to the floor or out the window. In this fashion you subtly reinforce your attention value for your listener. When you listen

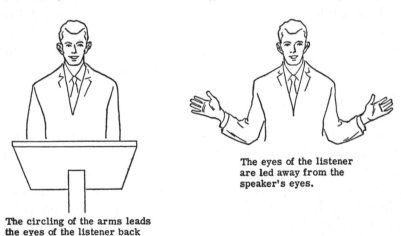

The eyes of the listener are led away from the speaker's eyes.

The circling of the arms leads the eyes of the listener back to the eyes of the speaker.

Fig. 4-2. An example of the posture lines.

to someone attentively, you watch his eyes. A speaker should never stand in such a way that the lines of his body pull the attention of his watching listener away from his eyes. As Cicero once remarked, they are the "windows of the soul."

The stereotype of the good speaker, then, will certainly include these three things:

1. The good speaker has eye contact with his listeners. He looks at them directly while he speaks.
2. The good speaker *leans into* the situation, actively giving and sharing his ideas and his enthusiasm with his listeners.
3. The good speaker stands or sits with his hands and arms easily relaxed in front of him or at his sides, being careful to avoid the awkwardness and distraction of body lines which pull the listener's eyes away from his own.

Other than these three suggestions, probably no rules are really needed. If you are leaning in, for example, the weight will be on the balls of the feet, not on one heel. If your hands and arms are forming effective focus-lines for you, you will not have your arms folded—or your hands on your hips, in your pockets, behind your back, or clasped solemnly across your abdomen. If you have good eye contact, you will not be staring at the ceiling, the floor, out the window, or at the back wall of the room. It is better to think positively. *Anything* you can do that will help you have better eye contact, establish a more direct interaction with your listeners, or keep their attention focused upon you—and especially upon your face and eyes—anything which can help you do these things is *good*.

The gestures of the good speaker

Gestures are of two kinds: *descriptive* and *enforcing*. They should grow out of the ideas you present rather than be superimposed upon them. In other words, it is not sensible to ask yourself, "Where shall I use a gesture?" Your concern should be instead, "How can I emphasize this idea?" or "How can I make this shape or size or action more vivid?" If you are an inactive speaker, try to include materials requiring you to point, or to describe, or to act out—but do not try to figure out ways to *gesture*.

A gesture has three essential parts: the preparation, the stroke, and the release. If any of them is weak or incomplete, the gesture will probably count for little—may even count against you.

If you are attending to the three rules for good presence, it will be easier for you to gesture. When you are leaning on a speaker's stand, it takes a good bit of time and energy to get your hands and arms sufficiently disentangled to move—the moment for the stroke may have passed. A good suggestion is to keep your hands free to gesture, and then you can do so when you want to.

The stroke of the gesture should reinforce your words, and therefore it should never take place outside what we might call the *visual square*. When you watch a speaker, as we have already seen, you focus upon his eyes. A movement below his belt line somewhere—or too far to the side, or too high—will distract your gaze to this new point and break your concentration. As is shown in Figure 4-3, however, a gesture which takes place between the speaker's eye level and his belt level, and no further to the side than the width of his shoulders, will be seen and evaluated without causing the listener to break eye contact. When the speaker wishes to point to something at his far right or far left, below his belt line or above his eye line, he simply *looks* at his own gesture, thus naturally shifting the visual square for the listener so that the eye contact can stay constant.

Fig. 4-3. The visual square.

An old rule of the theatre is that one should gesture with the upstage hand. This is a good rule for the speaker, too. As you gesture with your right hand, in other words, turn your body slightly to the right so the stroke of the gesture will take place in a plane with your eyes, or slightly behind them. If the stroke is to take place between your eyes and the audience rather than to one side, shift the weight of your body toward the gesture—thus seeming to *lean in* more, and adding to the force of the gesture.

All of this advice can be justified by the three principles noted before. The eyes of the listener seek the eyes of the speaker, and the gesture lines can distract or reinforce this effort at contact. Movement, of course, automatically attracts attention. We must be very careful that the deliberate movements we make with our hands and arms are not distracting attention from our essential message but are instead reinforcing the impact of that message upon the intelligence and feelings of those who hear us. Gestures must take place within the visual square to be effective. By letting his eyes follow his gesture, the speaker can safely alter the position of the square to his own advantage.

One should not discourage the gestures that children make when they speak. One should encourage them, instead, showing them how to control their gestures and make them full and meaningful. Even the littlest ones can be taught to move with grace rather than with awkwardness, to stand with calm poise rather than to slouch or stiffen, and to look at the class when they speak. If speech is made "fun," and suggestions rather than criticisms are made, much of the stagefright which so plagues adolescents and adults can be minimized or even eliminated. Older children, of course, can be taught the same basic principles of good presence which you are learning.

Summary

The bodily action of a speaker is an important contributor to his effectiveness. As a speaker, the teacher should remember that his essential purpose is to influence his hearers in some fashion. He will therefore want to establish a close, direct interaction between himself and his listening students. This will require eye contact, and a physical presence which suggests warm, friendly enthusiasm and the desire to share ideas. The basic posture should reinforce this impression, as should the gestures.

It is said that someone once asked Demosthenes what was the secret of his tremendous effectiveness as a speaker, and he replied, "Action!" When we are physically inactive, we lose a major source of our effectiveness. The listener reacts to our voice, to our appearance, and to our words. The good teacher consciously uses all three with effectiveness and care.

STUDY QUESTIONS

1. Why is posture important in speaking?

2. Why is it impossible to develop an effective single set of rules concerning posture and gesture?

3. What important principle of the painter can be applied by the speaker to help him gain and maintain attention?

4. Describe a good base posture for a person speaking, whether standing or sitting.

5. Define eye contact. What is its importance?

6. Why does the good speaker *lean into* the speaking situation?

7. Explain the two kinds of gestures, giving examples of each.

8. What are the three essential parts of a gesture?

9. Define the *visual square*.

10. Why should the speaker's eyes follow his gesture?

SUGGESTED ACTIVITIES

1. Present a brief pantomime to the class. Try to make your classmates understand your story from your gestures, movements, and facial expressions. Keep your task simple, like "decorating a Christmas tree," "feeding a baby," or "having a dog do tricks." Embroider upon the original situation, however, so you are telling a story. Perhaps the little children sneak downstairs while you are trimming the tree, and you

have to shoo them back up; or the phone rings while you are feeding the baby—anything. When you have finished, see how much of the story your classmates can reconstruct. Your whole purpose is to prove to yourself the power of visual communication, and to help you "unfreeze" a bit in front of others.

2. Imagine yourself in a formal situation, such as the annual "New Teachers" banquet in your community. Introduce one of your classmates to the group as a new teacher coming into your school. As you give your little talk, check your voice, diction, and expressiveness, of course, but concentrate on your presence, and upon that inevitable final gesture which will come as you turn to the person introduced. Remember to establish good eye contact, and to follow your gestures with your own eyes. Lean *in,* and keep your arm lines circling *inward*—constantly refocusing our attention upon your eyes.

SUPPLEMENTARY MATERIALS

Cheeseman, Grace, "The Concept of Naturalness as a Basis for Criticism," *Quarterly Journal of Speech,* Vol. XI, February 1925. This article is a classic on the subject, and is still both informative and challenging, even though written over a generation ago.

Dickens, Milton, *Speech: Dynamic Communication,* New York: Harcourt, Brace and Company, Inc., 1954, Chapter 7, "Bodily Communication." A well-written treatment of the subject from a more standard point of view, profusely illustrated with wonderfully revealing photographs.

5

Materials and their arrangement

Despite the evidence of some conversations you may be able to recall, it actually *is* impossible to talk without talking about *something*! In the classroom, where the usual purpose is to inform or to explain, it is especially important that there be care in the use of developmental materials and caution in the structuring of their presentation.

The human mind is trained to pay attention more easily to some kinds of things than it does to others. For example, we all listen more readily to the details of a story than we do to the details of a statistical report. As teachers, we need to learn to respect the inherent values of various kinds of materials and to make better uses of them in our teaching. We need to encourage our students to use a variety of materials in their reports, to test their evidence, and to feel free to share their experiences.

We also need to watch our patterning of our ideas. Experimental evidence pretty well agrees that we are more likely to attend to and remember something which we evaluate as being clearly organized than we are to something we evaluate as disordered or aimless.* All the oral skill that can be imagined will go for nothing if we cannot use it to put ideas across. The whole purpose of using the voice, of having clear diction, expressiveness, and effective personal appearance is to help us channel our message clearly to our listener. Basic to all speaking is content.

Using developmental materials

There is no list of developmental materials which may be considered as absolute. The length of the list, and the variety of its entries, depends upon which author you read. By and large, however, materials seem to group pretty well under five headings.

The first of these categories, in the sense that it is probably the commonest, includes that group of materials which we might call *examples*. This heading covers the detailed narrative illustration, the humorous anecdote, and the briefly cited instance. Probably next most frequent is *explanatory material*. In addition to explanations, this category includes descriptions—which explain appearances and space relationships just as explanations themselves usually concern logical relationships and time sequences. Definitions, too, would come in this category. Also common is the *quotation*. Sometimes the quote is from literature, at other times it is expert or ordinary testimony. It may even be vaguely cited gossip or hearsay. *Audio-visual supports,* and *statistics* form the last two categories—less frequently used, and more technical in nature.

We judge the usefulness of available material by its relevance, its reliability, and its potential result. It is a temptation, after having read on some topic in detail, to include *all* that we know instead of only that which is going to be directly helpful, but this temptation must be resisted if our classroom speech is to be effective. Relevancy of material is especially difficult to maintain. You

* Jon Eisenson, *The Psychology of Speech* (New York: Appleton-Century-Crofts, Inc., 1938), p. 217.

have all had classes with teachers who could not keep on the track. A digression, of course, may be worthwhile, but it should be channeled or cut off before it gets too far afield. Digressions, however, are not the only problem where relevancy is concerned. The increasing pile up of illustrations to make a single point may confuse rather than clarify. A welter of unclassified facts may so fog over the real purpose you have in mind that your students "lose sight of the woods for the trees."

Reliability is not always easy to check, but we owe it to ourselves and to our students to check as closely as we can. Unfortunately, we are not always aware of what we do *not* know, and unwittingly we sometimes pass on error. If you are using the kind of developmental material which comes from research, of course the evaluation of reliability is somewhat simplified. Who is the authority quoted? How does he know? When did he say or write this? These are questions which can generally be answered. If the material is from your own observation, however, the problem is quite different. Are you objective? Are you qualified to observe and judge these matters? We are all familiar with the casual tourist who forms firm opinions about the social, political and economic problems of some region which he briefly visits. Such "horseback judgments" are, of course, to be avoided. We are, however, also likely to assume the pose of an expert on matters of our daily routine when we may not be qualified to do so. Again, we are familiar with the farmer who knows *all* about farming, the teacher who knows *all* about teaching, the parent who knows *all* about children. It is humbling to remember that only God knows all, but it may help our accuracy as communicators! The good teacher is not afraid to say, "So far as I know."

Even though a particular quotation or illustration is relevant, and even though it creates a reliable image, it still may be unwise to use it. There is a great deal that could be said on almost any topic. The poor student, answering a question, tells you everything he can think of which is in any way related to the question you have asked. The good student, however, selects from among the relevant, reliable things he might say, choosing only those things which will be most likely to affect his listener. In the month of February, for example, almost all teachers will say something about Washington and Lincoln. What the first grade teacher chooses to say, however, should not be the same as what the seventh grade civics teacher chooses. The probable results—interest, understanding, application—these things help determine what is good content.

Example materials are useful for many reasons, but they are especially useful if your problem is to interest or to clarify. Whenever a story is begun, or some concrete image summoned to the mind's eye, listening becomes easier. A well-illustrated point will be remembered better than one which is simply stated. Which makes the idea more clear and vivid for you, the story of the boy who cried, "Wolf," or the statement that men will learn not to believe a liar; the story of the prodigal son, or the statement that parental love is strong? The answer is obvious. Dale Carnegie has said that the magic words of successful speaking are, *for example.*

Examples have power for several reasons. One is probably their specific nature. Whether the example is real or hypothetical, from experience or from literature, humorous or compelling, detailed or only briefly cited, direct or implied, it will summon up a specific concept rather than a general one. Another reason for their power is that examples so often are concrete rather than abstract. If the speaker can make his hearer see, taste or touch, hear or smell some specific thing, he will automatically compel attention and interest more than if he cannot. A third reason for the power of many examples is that they fall into narrative form. We are all of us almost inherently interested in how things come out. We listen even to dull jokes without changing the television dial until *after* the punch line. We watch even a bad drama long enough to be able to finish the story to our own satisfaction before we turn it off. The form itself has the power to compel.

Explanatory materials usually describe, enumerate, classify— sometimes even narrate. Example materials forward the progress of a speech, however, and explanatory materials do not. In a sense, explanatory materials are things you must say *before* you can make

your point. You have to describe the layout of a farm before you
can give instructions as to how the sand table is to be arranged;
you have to define *Pilgrim* before you can tell the story of
America's first settlement; you have to explain the way a case
comes before the United States Supreme Court before you can
have a class discussion of the implications of a recent decision.

Definitions are a special kind of explanation designed to give
meaning to a term. Explanations as such—and descriptions, too—
deal with the total statement of something; definitions deal with
a single word. Definitions are of various types; but, like all explanatory materials, they serve as a background for the consideration of
a point, rather than as a legitimate development of the point itself.
The biggest difficulty with such materials is that the speaker bogs
down in them, and never really gets to his point or his development.
They are hard to keep clear, hard to organize, and hard to keep
interesting. Obviously they are often necessary, but they should
be kept as brief as possible, and should always be carefully thought
out.

Quoted materials are extremely varied. It is important to remember here that—aside from literary quotation—the authority is of just
as great importance as the statement. After all, a thing is not *true*
simply because someone says it is, even if it is said in print! When
we substitute another's judgment for our own, we should be prepared to qualify the author of the statement to the listener just as
we would expect to qualify ourselves. Just as we would say, "When
I was in Mexico this past summer," so we should say, "According
to Dr. Henry Jones of the Spanish Department at State University,
who has just returned from a year of study in Mexico . . ." In
either case, the qualifications of "who said that?" are vital.

In some cases the date of the statement is crucial; in other cases
it is not. When telling elementary age children about Lincoln, for
example, it is enough to say, "Mrs. Lincoln wrote in one of her
letters." If you cite the same information in a college history class
paper, however, you had better give the date of the letter and
complete information as to where you found it.

Quotations are often singularly apt, and, when they are, should be used. If another's words say what you want said with special forcefulness—or beauty or clarity—by all means cite your source and use the quotation. Avoid, however, the random sprinkling of your remarks with frequent and unnecessary snatches of poetry, epigrams, and the like. Good quotations are undeniably excellent developmental devices; stilted, weak, or inappropriate quotations, however, are insufferable.

Statistical materials are almost universally and automatically thought of as dull. Obviously this dullness is not always present. The lecturer in history who piles casualty figure on casualty figure brings new meaning to the horror of the Civil War. Statistics, however, best follow examples or explanations; they should rarely if ever be used alone. It *is* true, of course, that sometimes there comes a point when nothing will satisfy the listener's intellectual curiosity other than actual figures—but, as a rule, figures should be sparingly used.

Audio-visual materials will be discussed in detail in a later chapter on demonstrations, but need to be mentioned here to complete our consideration. Such materials are all too often neglected as teaching aids, yet they are wonderful attention getters, have proved themselves experimentally to aid both comprehension and recall, and have the additional advantage of giving the speaker something to do with his hands.

The "natural orders" of material

Have you ever stopped in a strange town to ask directions, and been more baffled than helped by what you were told? As the confusing sequence continues—"three blocks this way, two blocks that. You can't miss it!"—you work with all the energy you can muster. You ask a few questions, you repeat bits of the advice to check them, and you may even draw an impromptu map on the back of an envelope. All of these efforts are made in the hope of giving order to something which seems to lack it. If your efforts are successful, you will reach your destination. If not, you will have to stop and ask again. The mind seeks order, and when it is not apparent, the mind strives consciously to make some order out of whatever is before it. When the process becomes too difficult, however, the mind gives up in frustration or disinterest, and wanders off to consider other things.

So it is with students in a class. As you tell them what you want them to learn, their minds will seek order in what you say. If they cannot find it, they will give up.

There are several orders which we use more or less regularly. Probably the commonest of these are the time sequence, the space sequence, the topical sequence, and the logical sequence.

In one sense, all sequences are *topical*. We have some main idea we wish to put across, and we present different aspects of it in order to develop it or prove it. In class, for example, your main idea might be the way in which animals can be thought of in families; and the topics would be the various families which you wanted to consider.

When contrasted with the time sequence, the space sequence, or the logical sequence, however, the topical sequence as such is unique. In it there is no special reason to take up any one topic before taking up another. In all of the other sequences the order of topics is predetermined by the relationships called for by the sequence itself. For example, when the topics are arranged in chronological order, we use the term, *time sequence*; when they are in the order of their space relationship to one another, *space sequence*. When the sequence shows cause and effect, or offers *reasons for* something, or attempts to prove a point, we say it is a *logical sequence*. Other sequences are *topical*.

Time sequences are generally narrative in form. The biographical material you give about an author whose work you are reading would be in time order, as would the oral report of one of your students on what he saw at the circus. The pattern, if it is orderly, will put the first things first, and then take up the next things, then the next, and so on until the story is completed. Sometimes the narrative is more specialized, in that it gives the steps in a process: first you do this, then you do this, then this, and last of all this. When you relate an experience, tell a story, give historical background, sketch in the facts about someone's life, give instructions, or read a recipe, you are using a time sequence. Words which characterize time sequences are words like *first, second, last of all, and then, afterwards, begin by,* and so on.

A space sequence is essentially a description. Common examples are giving directions about how to find something or someplace, describing your room, explaining the layout of your building, and so on. The space sequence uses words such as *in front, in back, at the left, at the right, above, below, the first thing you see,* and the like. Sometimes a space sequence becomes clearest when it is based upon a comparison, as when the street plan for Washington, D.C., is compared to the hub and spokes of a wheel, or the shape of Michigan's lower peninsula is compared to a mitten, with its thumb.

The logical sequence almost always uses or implies the word *because.* "Soil conservation practices are essential," we might say, and then go on to offer reasons. "The habit of thrift is a valuable one," we state, encouraging our students to purchase United States Savings Stamps on Stamp Day.

The purely topical sequence, almost without exception, takes one of the two forms of analysis: classification or division. The example already given concerning the various families in the animal kingdom will probably be dealt with as a problem in classification, taking a series of individual instances and grouping them under headings. Division, on the other hand, takes a single main head and breaks it into parts. What were the four most important causes of the fertility of the fields of our Midwestern corn belt, we ask a seventh grade geography class, and our resulting discussion follows a form of division—topical sequence.

These four sequences are usable and identifiable. You will use them, and, with your help, your students will also—to your mutual benefit, for the results will be greater clarity, and a more easily remembered presentation.

Summary

Whether you are reading, writing, speaking, or listening, you will find yourself, consciously or unconsciously, involved in matters of content and sequence. No communication can take place without examples, explanatory materials, quotations, statistics, or visual supports, and there can be no clear presentation of these materials without putting them into some kind of orderly sequence. Thought patterns are reflected in communication patterns, and communication patterns, in turn, reveal thought patterns. Cultivate the habit of checking your materials carefully, and of keeping them in a clear and sensible order. The good use of content and the various sequences of ideas will make you a better teacher. Teaching your students these same techniques will make *them* better students.

STUDY QUESTIONS

1. What are the three suggested criteria for judging whether or not certain content materials will be useful to the speaker's purpose?

2. What are the principal kinds of example materials discussed? What are their uses?

3. What are the principal kinds of explanatory materials discussed? What are their uses?

4. What are some things to consider in using a quotation? In using statistics?

5. What do we mean when we say that there are *natural orders* of material?

6. In what sense are all sequences of ideas *topical*? In contrast to this general concept, what is the nature of the true topical sequence as such?

7. What are some of the commonest kinds of time sequences? What is likely to be wrong with them?

8. What are some of the commonest kinds of space sequences? What are some words which show space relationship?

9. What is the purpose of the logical sequence? What words are usually stated or implied?

10. Distinguish between *classification* and *division*.

SUGGESTED ACTIVITIES

1. Prepare on little slips of paper a series of simple suggested topics which would require a speaker to use time or space sequences. Examples might be

How do you go home from here?
How are the parts of a business letter arranged on a page?
How is a place setting correctly arranged at the dinner table?
How do you drive a car?

After the teacher has checked over all of the topics, put them face down on a desk or table. Have everyone in the class, in turn, draw three slips. Immediately after drawing, choose one of the slips, put the other two back, announce your topic, and speak. Have the listeners rate the sequences given as *clear* or *confusing*, and give you their unsigned comments. In this way you can see just how clear you were.

2. Prepare an analysis of a speech which you read in a recent issue of *Vital Speeches Magazine*, listing all the content materials the speaker uses. Decide which kind he uses most, and speculate in a paragraph or so as to why this might be the case.

3. On some assigned subject, such as "reading," "education," "teaching as a profession," prepare a brief outline for each kind of sequence. Remember, use the *same* subject—finding a time sequence related to it, a space sequence, a topical sequence, and a logical sequence. What kind of content materials would you be most likely to use in each case?

SUPPLEMENTARY READINGS

Brigance, W. Norwood, *Speech: Its Technique and Disciplines in a Free Society*, New York: Appleton-Century-Crofts, Inc., 1952, pp. 212-224, most of a fine chapter on "Organizing the Speech into Orderly Form." The orders are thought of under slightly different headings, but the examples and sample outlines are excellent.

Bryant, Donald C., and Karl R. Wallace, *Fundamentals of Public Speaking*, New York: Appleton-Century-Crofts, Inc., 1947, pp. 89-103 of Chapter 6, "The Psychological Bases of the Speaker's Task."

This material was omitted from the later revision of the book, but for our purposes is uniquely useful. The diagrams showing The Laws of Familiarity and Pattern are especially helpful.

McCall, Roy C., *Fundamentals of Speech*, New York: The Macmillan Company, 1949, Chapter V. A definitive, thorough chapter on the subject. Although McCall's basic headings are a bit different from the ones we have used, his examples and clarity of presentation add to our understanding.

section two

Classroom speaking: the teacher's speech

There is probably good reason to argue that teachers use all kinds of speaking in the classroom, but there are some kinds which are used more often and more generally than others. It can be demonstrated, for example, that all teachers make explanations, have class discussions, and hold individual conferences. Most teachers work demonstrations into their lesson plans from time to time, and story-telling of one kind or another, as well as oral reading, seems common enough to merit special consideration.

The purpose of this section is not to cover all there is to know about speech, but instead to give you some background for six kinds of speaking which you will unquestionably use. These kinds of speaking may be thought of as tools, and your careful study of them can help you achieve your professional desire to be stimulating, clear, and helpful in the classroom.

6

Reading aloud

All of us who teach find ourselves from time to time cast in the role of the interpretative reader. Since most people do not read very well, this thought is not a particularly comforting one. There are, however, a few basic rules which any reader can follow if he would improve his ability to read meaningfully and vividly.

When we read aloud, we must first of all concern ourselves with the mood and the meaning of someone else—the writer. Only insofar as we understand him can we project his ideas and feelings to others. When we read aloud we must also concern ourselves with the reactions and responses of our listeners. Only insofar as we communicate with them can we justify our speaking at all. The oral reader, in other words, has but a single purpose: to relate the meaning and feeling of the writer to the needs and interests of the listener.

Choosing materials

The first considerations in choosing material for oral reading should be your purpose and your audience. One does not just read, he reads something to someone for some reason. After all, why should it ever be more sensible to read aloud than to talk or to tell? Because in some cases written materials have precision or delight which cannot be matched in paraphrase. The power of a Supreme Court decision, the exactness of a statistical analysis, the beauty of a sonnet by Shakespeare, the charm and wit of a passage from Lewis Carroll—these qualities cannot be ignored.

If the material to be read is expository, it should be clear, precise, exact, accurate, and authoritative. The reading should be preceded by a brief statement qualifying its writer and showing its relevance to the point at hand. In some cases the exact source should be given, perhaps even including the date of the publication. Expository materials are usually read to prove something, and therefore the recency, reliability, and relevancy of the material must be established.

If the material is narrative, however, these matters do not apply. When choosing narrative materials, you should first of all determine the theme. Even in the case of story-hour selections for the early grades, the theme should be clear and vital. A dull, or undefined theme will lead to a weak story. The plot should be strong, active, and vigorous. With children, heroes must have obstacles to overcome, problems to resolve, difficulties to conquer. Good must triumph. With older listeners, the story must have cleverness, or humor, or suspense—or perhaps a sense of nostalgia or moving beauty. There should be a strong message; a meaning as well as a mood. Characters should be unique and worth thinking about. Even though fanciful, they should have one foot in reality, and be well-drawn. The dialog should be forceful and direct—never "cute" or laden with "fine-writing." A good story will rise or fall with its plot, its theme, its characters. These three main elements must be judged and understood by the reader or he will not be able to motivate them adequately for his listeners.

If the material is humorous, you should judge your audience and occasion with especial care. Suitability, appropriateness, standards of good taste—all such matters are of real importance. "When in doubt, leave it out," is probably a good rule to follow. If you are not sure whether or not something will go over, you will have trouble with it, and be self-conscious about using it. Choose something else.

If the material is poetic, be sure that you like it yourself. For that matter, do not ever read anything simply because you "think you should." Especially avoid this sort of performance in poetry. Whimsical verse has fragility which your lack of sympathy can destroy; while serious verse has a power which cannot come out unless you are responsive enough to release it. Check the poem to be sure that it is oral, with warmth and concreteness and a sense of uncluttered reality. Avoid the trite or the overdone, the sentimental, the insipid, and the merely cute unless there is a real reason for using them.

Preparing to read

Once material is found which is well-suited to your purpose, and you have decided to read rather than tell it, the next step is to prepare the selection for reading aloud. Be sure, first of all, that you have a full realization of the meaning of the writer. The good reader will analyze the material closely, grouping ideas and charting transitions with care. He will look for the climax, so he can build up to it effectively. He will mark awkward places, so the meaning can come out clearly—perhaps he will underline keywords or mark in a pause or a breath that will assist clarity.

After the material has been analyzed in this way, read it aloud all the way through, listening to yourself carefully as you go. This reading will give you some idea of what the delivery problems are, and your structural analysis will help you pin-point them even further. Check your pronunciation of any doubtful words, as well as the meaning of any unfamiliar ones. Practice the tongue-twister phrases until they hold no surprises. Search not only for meaning, but for mood. Here you may even want to do research, for the biographic, historical, or geographic background of the writer—the selection itself may add much to your intuitive insight. Be sure the theme is clear to you, so that you can project it clearly to others.

There is no one set of markings which is perfect, so work out your own; then you will have no trouble being sure what is meant. Mark especially key words and phrases for emphasis, key pauses, places where the mood insists upon softer or louder, faster or slower delivery. Put in warning signals to yourself about the tricky spots. Use colored pencils if you need to, and do not assume that you will remember anything. Mark it!

One last word about preparing the manuscript. You will probably want to begin a notebook of materials which you can use over and over again. As a general rule the print of the book itself will not give you room to mark things, and it may even be fine enough to cause you reading problems—especially if you wear glasses. Radio and television scripts are usually typed up in full capital letters, triple-spaced with extra space between paragraphs. This form is a real aid to the reader, and you may wish to adopt it.

Reading aloud

If you have chosen your material carefully, with due respect for the needs and interests of your listeners, and if you have done a good job of analyzing the material and preparing it for reading, the actual reading will be fairly easy to manage. Try to apply all that you have learned about voice, diction, expressiveness, and appearance. Remember that the audience will both listen and watch in order to understand.

The key word to keep in mind is probably *sharing*. As we listen to you read, you must project to us the feeling that you care about this selection for some reason. You are enthusiastic, or in dead earnest, or personally moved as a result of reading it yourself, and, as you read to us, something of this reaction must come through. Use facial expression and the general set of your posture to help you put across the meaning and the mood which you desire. Do not act, but try a few gestures if you feel they would help. Often a little suggestion of movement can add to your effectiveness, especially if well used, seemingly unstaged, and not done too frequently.

Remember above all that you are reading *to us*. You should know your material so well that you can look at us as you read. Let your eyes take in a phrase, then look up and tell it to us. Do not mumble into the book or bury your eyes in your manuscript.

Do not overplay the dramatic parts, or laugh too much at the humor of what you read. Remember that oral reading finds its power in suggestion. When the gestures are too large, or too many, when the voice is too theatrical or the diction too "stagy," suggestion cannot be in effect. Nothing is left to suggest! The image is chased away and the illusion is broken.

Impromptu reading

Teachers are sometimes forced to read when they have not had time to prepare. There is no substitute for the steps we have already considered, and an impromptu performance will probably not be as good as one which is well thought-out ahead of time. Elementary and pre-school teachers, however, cannot always permit themselves the luxury of careful analysis, marking a script, and oral practice for everything which they read aloud.

Even so, there are some things which can be done. You can, for example, take a quick look at the material to see what is involved. How long is it? Are there subheads and italicized topic sentences, or is it straight reading? Is there dialog? If there are any pictures, take a good look at them; they can sometimes tell you a lot about what you are getting into, and whether your touch should be light or somewhat heavier. Noting such matters can give you a quick preview of what is to come, at least in a general sense; and with this information you are somewhat better prepared to deal effectively with the meaning and mood of the selection.

When you read impromptu, use as much eye contact as you can. It will help if you keep your thumb or finger running down the page as you go along so you will not get lost. Read a little slower than usual, to give yourself time to be expressive. By looking up during the dialog, help the listeners know when one speaker leaves off and another begins. Indicate the punctuation as well as the words.

Some people become excellent impromptu readers, but it should be pointed out that these people are good readers *with* preparation as well as without. Preparation teaches what to look for and what to do. Experience will help you in time to develop some intuitive sense of readiness and ease, provided that you base your experience upon wise practices of careful preparation whenever possible. Impromptu reading, though sometimes necessary, is never to be regarded as desirable.

The student reader

Unfortunately, about the only oral reading most school children do is impromptu. This kind of reading experience is generally designed to test the child's reading vocabulary rather than to give him the opportunity to share meaning or mood. With some help from you, however, the pupils in your classes can learn to read expressively.

As a first step you must consider reading readiness. A child must be able to read silently with understanding before he can hope to be an effective oral reader. If he speaks in sentences, reads silently at the difficulty level of the material he would share, and is reasonably secure in his sense of belonging, there is no real reason why he cannot read effectively.

Let him use the same techniques you use. Help him to analyze the material first for its ideas; then let him read it aloud once to himself. The next step is more analysis—for mood, characterization, and sense of dialog. He should be encouraged to mark a few things, and—as he reads—he should look at his listeners as much as he can. Incidentally, remember to respond yourself to what he does, for *you* will be his most important listener.

As he grows older, this technique of silent analysis, oral survey, further analysis, marking, and practice will pay off for him again and again in the dividends of appreciation from his listeners. As his basic skill grows, his impromptu ability will also develop.

Summary

Good oral reading demands an awareness of the meaning and mood of the material, and of the needs and goals of the listeners. Like all communication, good oral reading is direct and personal. Good technique begins with a conscious choice of material, for oral reading is a purposive activity. The steps in preparation involve careful analysis and marking of the material, while effective delivery demands that the reader free himself of his personal inhibitions and project the full sense of the writer to his hearers. Even the "Minutes of the Meeting" can be read effectively and clearly! But not without thought. When good reading's prerequisites have been met often enough, impromptu skill will be found to have developed, too.

STUDY QUESTIONS

1. What is the purpose of the oral reader?
2. Suggest one or two ways in which reading aloud is basically like other forms of communication. What is the principal difference between reading and speaking to a listener?
3. What should be your first considerations in selecting material?
4. Why should some materials be read rather than told?
5. How should expository material be judged for readability?
6. What characteristics should a narrative have to make it suitable for oral reading?
7. How does one analyze a selection for meaning and mood? Suggest a few sorts of background research which might prove helpful.
8. Suggest three kinds of things which a reader might mark in his manuscript.
9. What are some characteristics of oral reading readiness?
10. What are the basic steps in preparing a selection for oral reading?

SUGGESTED CLASS ACTIVITIES

1. The problems of reading prose and poetry are different. Whether the selection is humorous or dramatic makes a difference which cannot be overlooked. Find an example of a short inspirational poem, a humorous ditty, an anecdote or quip which is in prose, and a bit of serious, dramatic prose. Read them to the class as examples of different styles of writing, and consider the problems these styles pose for the oral reader. Explain what each selection represents as you go along. If a tape recorder is available, use it so you may hear for yourself how well you were able to project mood and meaning.

2. Work up a short cutting from a play, using different classmates in different roles. Have each one explain first what the personality is which he is to portray, and how he will use his voice to put this characterization across.

SUPPLEMENTARY READINGS

Arbuthnot, May Hill, *Children and Books,* Chicago: Scott, Foresman and Company, 1957, pp. 16, 25-26, 196-206. Some excellent suggestions on reading aloud to children. Brief and pertinent.

Compere, Moiree, *et al., Curriculum Guide for High School Interpretation, 1958.* This little booklet was planned by a committee of the Michigan Speech Association, and is available through the Department of Speech at the University of Michigan, Ann Arbor. It includes many concrete suggestions for special units on oral reading in the High School, as well as bibliographies of books and recordings.

Ogilvie, Mardel, *Speech in the Elementary School,* New York: McGraw-Hill Book Company, Inc., 1954, Chapter 4, "Oral Reading." Some good notions on stimulating your children to read aloud *well* in class.

7

Story telling

A number of careful personality studies have been made which establish rather clearly the characteristics of a good teacher.* Among these characteristics is the ability to put people at ease—to give them a sense of well-being and belonging and worth. Among them also are the ability to be clear and the ability to be vivid—at times even compelling. One of the most frequently used tools designed to assist in the accomplishment of all these ends is the tool of story telling.

The kinds of stories you will use in your classroom, of course, depend a great deal upon the age of your students and the subject matter you will teach. For example, although they also use other

---

* Several of these studies are summed up in Seth Fessenden, *Speech and the Teacher* (New York: Longmans, Green and Co., Inc., 1949), pp. 4-20. See also Walter S. Monroe, ed., *The Encyclopedia of Educational Research* (New York: The Macmillan Company, 1950), "Teaching Competencies."

forms of narrative, the pre-school teacher and the teacher in the primary grades make a frequent use of folk tales of all kinds. As the age level of the students goes up, the stories shift from fantasy to fact, with the emphasis ultimately coming on anecdotes, illustrations, case studies, and historical narratives.

Regardless of the age group and the subject-matter being taught, there are a few suggestions which can be helpful.

Finding and using stories

The stories we tell in conversation usually arise out of what is being discussed. One thing leads to another, and we begin telling something that happened, or something we read, or saw, or heard. Some stories you will use in the classroom will "come to you" in much this same way—as you are talking. It is a good idea, however, to aid the process as much as you can. By this suggestion nothing manipulative is meant, simply that it is wise to become as good an observer and rememberer as possible. Our stories may be reports based on our own experiences, or they may be jokes, anecdotes, fables, or even story-tellers' tales. All can be useful in the classroom.

A primary source of the stories we use, of course, is our own experience. When we do observe something, there are only three kinds of things we can say about it. We can describe it; we can read into it cause or effect, or some other inferential relationship; or we can tell how it makes us feel. In other words, we can make objective, speculative, or judgmental statements about a thing, but that is all.

Unfortunately, we are not often aware of the kind of observations we are making, nor are we often careful about the kinds of statements we use. We make a judgment act as if it were a description, saying for example, "John is lazy." This statement does not *describe* John nearly so much as it *judges* him. It tells more about *our* standards for John's behavior than it tells about what John actually does.

It is difficult to relate an occurrence completely at the descriptive level. A woman unexpectedly runs across the street in front of our car. When we tell someone else about it, we will probably expand on the basic facts of the incident, offering possible causes, citing the dangers potentially in the situation, sharing with others our surprise and our fright. Our statements will be objective, speculative, judgmental, all three. A good teacher who was observant could use this simple incident as a well-told story to dramatize a safety lesson for little children; to make a point in a psychology class; to illustrate plot development in a high school English class; to serve as the basis for a "stock" journalism assignment, *ad infinitum!* But, if not really observed and remembered, the incident becomes just one more episode in a lifetime.

The really good observer learns to get the facts before he makes speculative statements or uses value judgments. "John turned in six assignments late during the first half of the term. He does not use his study hall time to study. He checks no books out of the library." These are objective statements. "John is not interested in the course. He does not seem to have any sense of goal in his work. Perhaps he gets too little encouragement at home, or has to work too many outside hours on a part-time job to do good school work." These are speculative statements. "John is a likable person, easy-to-know and friendly. John is worth 'saving' in the course, in spite of his poor record." These are judgmental statements. If we were to tell the story of John's problems with his school-work to help us make a point, we would need to use all three kinds of statements. To be a good story teller, in other words, we must be alert enough to observe the facts, creative enough to speculate concerning their causes and effects, responsive enough to make judgments, and sharp enough to carry all kinds of little stories and examples around in our heads, ready for instant use.

Jokes, anecdotes, and other brief narrative illustrations not based on personal experience are also helpful classroom tools. Think of the good teachers you have known. One reason they were good was because they always seemed to have an apt illustration they could call up to help them make a point. Sometimes their narrative examples were from familiar stories, sometimes they were humorous anecdotes, sometimes they were from the newspaper, or a recent television show. These people may have kept scrapbooks of good material they thought they might use someday—or they may simply have learned to make good mental notes. Taking your cue from their example, you should start making your collection now! Put in it good cartoons, little stories, bits of poetry—anything which might be useful to you someday to make spelling less painful or the study of civics more fun. Establish the habit of using these illustrations and sharing your observations regularly.

These informal kinds of story-telling, of course, are not the only ones used in the classroom. Almost every good teacher develops a few stories of a more formal type which he purposefully uses. A child is taught to read music with the help of a story about the family of notes who live in a "Staff House" with an upper and a lower floor. College history teachers tell fascinating true-stories of the events of the Civil War. A high school mathematics teacher tells his pupils the story of the development of numbers, and teaches them to use an abacus as has been done for centuries in the Orient. We hear the story of Pasteur in biology, and of Pavlov in psychology. In Latin, in literature, in history, and drama classes we read and study stories, and in physics, and geometry, and choral music, we hear other stories, brought in to give background and appreciation and understanding.

It does not matter that no two people learn and re-create stories in exactly the same way. What matters is that we develop a fund of materials we can draw on, deliberately or casually, to help us in the classroom. A good rule, actually, would be that each of us should learn from four to six stories every year. Soon we would have a fund of useful materials which could be of great value in our teaching.

The qualities of a good story

A story is, first of all, a time sequence. This means that it follows an order that is chronological. Any other order (the flashback, for example) automatically requires careful explanation and extra-clear telling.

The first few sentences are an introduction. They usually set the scene, introduce the characters, and suggest the theme which is to be dealt with. A good story has a *protagonist*, or hero, who has a problem or conflict to resolve. In the introduction we need to learn quickly just who the protagonist is, and what problem he faces. Think of the way in which the familiar story of "The Good Samaritan" begins, or of the "Once upon a time" beginnings of "The Three Bears" or "Little Red Riding-Hood." Who, what, when, where, and why get quickly answered, and then the story is on its way. Whether a joke or a folk tale, this kind of beginning is typical of the good story.

The development of the story must have both narrative and dialog. The language must be appropriate to the characters and to the story itself. The Three Little Pigs, for example, or Chicken-Little, do not talk like Sleeping Beauty. Neither do *any* of the folk-tale characters talk like the "real" little boys and girls who speak in a story from true experience. There should not be many characters, and the plot should not be too complicated. The story is oral, after all, and the listener does not want to clutter up his mind with too many details. The plot line should have action, and it should stick with the original note of trouble which was sounded in the introduction. This is the "big idea" of the whole story, and it should be built up steadily until it reaches a final moment of climax when things are resolved one way or another— or the "punch line" is given. A good story has a clarity of characterization, a unity of interest, and an economy of events which will make the suspense of its development and the power of its climax recognizable, logical, and pleasurable to all who hear it.

The conclusion is usually handled with much the same sort of dispatch that is characteristic of the introduction. "And so they were married and lived happily ever after," the fairy tale concludes; "and the big, bad wolf never bothered them again," ends "The Three Little Pigs"; and so on. The whole point of the conclusion is to end things satisfactorily. There is no need to moralize, as a rule; if the story has been apt and well-told, the lesson will be taught without the dullness of added preachment.

Telling the story

A story, of course, must be adapted to the needs of an audience. Stories can be introduced to children too young, or, for that matter, they can be too juvenile or too unsophisticated for the older listener. As a story teller you must "put yourself in the other fellow's shoes," or your story may do your cause more harm than good. One group of college students will never forget a compulsory chapel which they attended a few years back, because their school's president—before their incredulous eyes—in all seriousness insisted upon telling the entire story of *The Little Engine that Could* to make his point. After some five or ten minutes of laborious "I think I can, I think I can," the student body evidently decided the whole thing was a burlesque, and joined in. Joyously they sent the little train down the mountain, chanting "I thought I could, I thought I could, I thought I could," with all the verve of a varsity cheer. As a result the poor president lost all track of his point, and concluded in confusion. To him the experience was entirely unnerving. The point for us, of course, is that we should not misgauge our audience!

You should be careful, also, not to wax too dramatic. There is a real but subtle difference between acting and story telling—a difference which, if not respected, can cause painful embarrassment to the audience. You should, of course, use as agreeable a voice as you can, as flexibly as possible, with clear, pure diction. There is no special voice for telling stories, and this kind of affectedness can be labeled with only one term—repulsive! There are many fine recordings of great actors and actresses doing scenes from great plays, or reading from literature. Listen to them and study how they recreate the sense of "expanded conversation" in their tone, yet still manage to convey the widest possible range of emotion.

You should watch your audience as you talk, and be ready yourself to respond to *their* responses. Do they seem puzzled—straighten them out, and then go on. Use enough gestures to hold interest, but do not "saw the air" too much. Be careful not to dress in such a way that people cannot forget what you have on, and be careful, also, not to use such fascinating pictures and objects that your words become unnecessary and anticlimactic.

For the formal stories you tell, learn the details in order, and polish up your beginnings and endings. What is so lame as the joke which begins, "Well, there was this man and he . . . ," and what is so frustrating as a forgotten punch-line? Practice aloud, and remember that what you practice is what you will learn to do well—so do not let yourself stop and start. Go right on as if the audience were there. If you talk yourself out on a limb, talk yourself off of it again. For the informal stories, learn to observe and remember. The only practice is conversation. Try a joke, an anecdote or two, a shared experience. There is no way to learn to tell stories well except by learning and telling them.

The student story teller

As a teacher you will find that story telling is an extremely helpful self-development technique for your students to use. The "sharing time" of the little child is, after all, a story-telling period. In a sense, so is the book review or current events period in a junior high class, or the assigned oral report sequence of a senior seminar in college. Try to help your pupils keep their time sequences in order and to learn to respond to their audiences. These are the two main things. Help them to keep good voice and diction, and appropriate expressiveness. Do not encourage the theatrical or affectedly elocutionary kinds of performance.

All the points in this chapter which apply to you as the teacher will also apply to your students later on. Your technique with them should be, of course, to encourage, not compel; to reward, not penalize.

Summary

The good story is a clear time sequence. It has unity of theme, action, believable suspense, a sense of climax, and an economy of detail. It should be told with gestures and vocal variety, but also with a sense of restraint lest it become ridiculous.

The good story teller is a good observer. He knows how to make objective statements, and how to speculate and make value judgments concerning them. He is, in other words, creative and original.

Telling a story to someone is a "reaching out" to them—a sharing of yourself and your ideas which is unique and heart-warming. Learn to observe things about you. Narrative is based on observation—as is expressiveness, also. Make it a habit to develop little webs of speculation about what you see. Why is this true? What is that like? Such questions lead to the beginnings of stories, anecdotes, illustrations which can help your teaching, because they will make it real and personal. The good teacher works narrative into his speaking and teaching regularly. Behind the finished product, however, are some concrete steps of preparation:

1. Know the story well. Polish up the introduction and conclusion especially. Keep it moving, and do not let *yourself* lose interest, or the recital will sag.
2. Keep the time sequence clear. Do not digress, or bring in details until you are ready for them. Plan the tale so that it is as uncomplicated as possible.
3. Relate the story directly, forthrightly, and as interestingly and vividly as you can.

Other than these suggestions, the only technique useful is the technique of sharing—a technique which implies a pride in the act and a friendly sense of willingness. Without these qualities, all techniques will fail.

STUDY QUESTIONS

1. What are the three kinds of statements we can make about anything we may observe? Give an example of each.
2. Distinguish between *formal* and *informal* story-telling.
3. How can the good observer use his observation in the classroom?

4. Explain the way in which a story is, first of all, a time sequence.

5. Characterize the introduction of a story. What should it include?

6. How does the development of the plot relate to the introduction?

7. What is the essential purpose of the conclusion?

8. What are two or three things to watch when telling a story? Explain the importance of each.

9. How should the story be rehearsed? Why?

10. Define a *good story*.

SUGGESTED CLASS ACTIVITIES

1. Go to some place on the campus, or in the community, and observe for one minute. Jot down notes on everything you see, hear, or in any other way experience. From the facts you gather, or some of them at least, speculate and evaluate until you can form a story. For example, watch the traffic at a busy corner. Could you make a story out of what you see which would teach a safety lesson? Could you make a story which would illustrate the point that, although "the lights change" from time to time, "the stream of life" goes on? Could you make a story which would teach us something by analogy about the ebb and flow of business cycles? Observe, speculate, evaluate, apply! Keep your story short—a minute or so is fine. Be prepared to tell it in class.

2. Select a hypothetical classroom situation and be prepared to tell about it. Then, with your classmates pretending to be the pupils in the class you have outlined, tell a story. Learn it carefully, and tell it expressively. When you have finished, discuss together how suitably the story was chosen and told for the imaginary group.

3. Learn and rehearse a good joke which can be used to illustrate a point. State the point to the class and then tell the story, just as you might in the development of a speech or a classroom lecture. Keep it brief, and do not forget the punch line! Remember, also, the standards of good taste which apply to the classroom, and the age level of the students for whom you intend the joke.

SUPPLEMENTARY MATERIALS

Arbuthnot, May Hill, *Children and Books*, Chicago: Scott, Foresman and Company, 1957, Chapter 12, "Using Folk Tales With Children." This book is a classic in its field, and this chapter is filled with helpful suggestions.

Ogilvie, Mardel, *Speech in the Elementary School*, New York: McGraw-Hill Book Company, Inc., 1954, pp. 134-138, "Storytelling." Well thought-out suggestions for helping the children in your classrooms develop this useful art.

Sawyer, Ruth, *The Way of the Storyteller*, New York: Viking Press, 1957, p. 131 ff, "A Technique to Abolish Technique." A master story teller gives a few tips on how it is done. Do not expect any formulae, however, for Miss Sawyer's art is intuitive and personal. This book contains a fine collection of folk-tales and the like, especially for telling.

Siks, Geraldine Brain, *Creative Dramatics: An Art for Children*, New York: Harper & Bros., 1958. A frequent outgrowth of story-telling in the lower grades is the experience of creative play-making. This and the Ward book are extremely helpful on this subject.

Tooze, Ruth, *Storytelling*, Englewood Cliffs, N. J.: Prentice-Hall, Inc., 1959. Of the same type as the Sawyer book, but in some ways clearer.

Ward, Winifred, *Playmaking with Children*, 2nd. ed., New York: Appleton-Century-Crofts, Inc., 1954.

8

Expository speaking

The primary task in teaching is to explain things. Sometimes the teacher's problem is to give new information; sometimes it is to clarify a process. But almost every time the teacher speaks in class he does so to explain something in some way. This job is not an easy one, for students are not trained listeners. In terms of their learning level, the material presented is often difficult. To make things even worse, the teacher is often untrained in the oral presentation of materials. It is important, therefore, that the teacher learn and regularly use good practices of oral exposition.

The listener

When one person listens to another person, he does more than just hear what is said. Listening takes energy because it implies understanding—or at least the effort to understand. The good speaker tries as best he can to minimize the amount of energy it will take the listener to hear and understand what he says. This means that he must use his best vocal production, his clearest articulation, the most appropriate bodily action possible, and so on. But it also means that he must pay careful attention to the formulation and structure of his ideas. When the speaker's delivery, his conception of his point, or his organizational pattern are fuzzily managed, the listener has to expend extra energy in order to understand—extra energy which he may be unwilling or even unable to give. When such extra effort on the part of the listener is required, all too often the result is that the teacher does not teach and the student does not learn.

One of the primary things a speaker can do to assist his listener is to be well organized. Organization is especially necessary for the teacher because he must not only be understandable and clear in the usual sense, but he must also, in many cases, be repeatable—word-for-word. As any grade school child can verify, it is one thing to *understand* how to do long division as he watches someone else do it, and quite another thing to *understand* long division well enough that he can work a problem for himself—or show someone else how to work one.

There are, however, several time-tested techniques which can help you to make your explanations both clear and, if need be, repeatable. In an earlier chapter we took up the use of content materials, and the inherent basic sequences in which ideas must be comprehended and expressed. In this chapter we will take up some of the applicable fundamentals of topic development and structure. In the last analysis, there are probably only three things over which the speaker really has much control: his delivery and use of language, his choice of content material, and his general organization. Even in these three there are limits upon what he can do. By applying good techniques carefully, however, the speaker can at least be sure of being reasonably clear.

Consider for a moment the kind of speeches the teacher usually gives in a classroom. Today, especially in the public schools, the formal lecture is rare. What the teacher usually does instead is to give a series of short explanations, using demonstrations and questions throughout, in order to drive his points home. All too often these little explanations-in-a-series fail, because the teacher is not able to express clearly enough what it is he wants to put across. At one time or another we have all experienced this inability to be clear about something. Sometimes it is the result of not having thought things out fully enough. We rush into speech, forgetting that before we can put an idea into words for others to understand, we must know its accurate dimensions ourselves. As a result we do not always put the things we want to say clearly enough, or in complete enough form for others to understand them.

The first step in clear exposition is to determine exactly what it is that you want to talk about. This step involves what we call *subject*, and what we call *topic*. A subject is a broad, general sort of thing—like The Multiplication Table, or Reading Musical Notes, while the topic is a narrower aspect of the subject as a whole.

You may decide early in the term, for example, that during November you will discuss with your class the settlement of America. Exactly what you will take up on the second Monday of the month at 10:00 a.m. is your topic for that time. What a teacher presents in class, then, is really a series of *topical* explanations, all grouped under one or another of several *subjects*.

The person who is asked to give a public speech is usually called upon for some specific reason which makes his choice of subject virtually automatic. For example, he is asked to speak before a Kiwanis Club because he is actively working in a certain job, profession, or industry which is important to the community, or of special interest to the club. In such a case, the speaker's subject is dictated by his own status, or authority, or experience. Or he is called upon to speak in behalf of the Red Cross before his P.T.A., in which case his subject is dictated by the nature of the occasion. In all of these cases, however, even though the *subject* is fixed, the *topic* remains to be decided by the speaker himself.

In teaching, a similar situation exists, although the subjects of the teacher's talks before his class are not fixed by quite the same factors. Here the academic discipline being taught and the grade level of the student affect the subject choices very rigidly. The selection of specific topics and their emphasis and ordering, however, even in the classroom are under the control of the individual teacher.

The thesis statement

Suppose that you are teaching a unit on natural science. Since a single unit can deal with only one phase of such a large subject, we will assume that this unit takes up the study of shellfish. But even Shellfish cannot serve as a topic for a specific day's lesson. When considered in relation to "Natural Science," "Shellfish" is

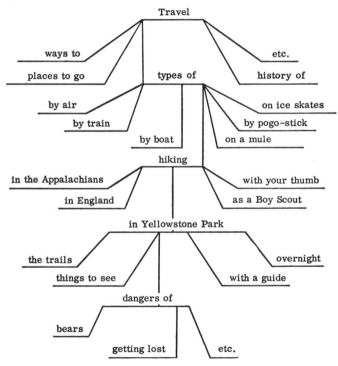

Fig. 8-1. The speaker's approach to choosing a topic. The speaker is planning to talk on the dangers of hiking in Yellowstone Park. His topic can be further broken down into subtopics, which he may choose to use as main divisions in his speech, depending on his purpose, the inherent basic sequence, and so on.

a topic; but when considered in relation to "Crabs" or "Clams," it becomes, by our previous definition, a subject! Schematically, then, almost anything which you might choose to discuss, with the possible exception of the vaguest and most all-inclusive of generalities, is simultaneously a subject and a topic, depending upon the point of view from which it is considered. The diagram shows the multiple possibilities a speaker has, and offers a suggestion of the manner in which a subject may be narrowed down to manageable topics.

Once a topic is determined, the speaker should then turn it into a one-sentence statement. This statement will imply, or better yet, specifically declare both *what he is going to talk about,* and *what he is going to say about it.* Such a statement is called a *thesis,* and has been in rhetorical use since the days of the ancient Greeks.

Sometimes we make the thesis a literal statement of topic and purpose:

> "I want to explain today how to set up the form of a business letter."
> "I want to explain and demonstrate for you the Pythagorean Theorem."
> "Today, children, we are going to learn how three new letters look, and what they say."

Sometimes we disguise or adapt the thesis, giving it more than the mere quality of statement alone:

> "How does a lovely blossom such as this one change and become a golden apple?"
> "The causes of the Civil War are not simple to explain, nor have they ever been clearly and definitely determined."
> "It is perspective which makes the artist's picture seem to come to life and have the dimension of depth."

In each of these cases, however, there is stated or clearly implied both topic and purpose for the talk. Toward the beginning of each explanation you make there should be some such statement—and most of the time you should probably keep it fairly literal.

If this kind of beginning seems pretty dull, remember that it serves the necessary function of alerting the listener to what it is he is expected to listen *for*. It is like looking up a word in the dictionary. If you know exactly how the word is spelled, it is a lot easier and quicker to find than if you only know that "it starts with an *s*."

The thesis pattern

Once the thesis is set, the next step in making a good explanation is to consider what you might possibly say to support it. This can probably be most easily determined by asking questions of your thesis, such as "Why?" "How?" "Under what conditions?" "Who says so?" and the like. Suppose your thesis is, "I want to tell you how to organize a good speech." The obvious question is, "Well, how do you do it?" and the answer becomes the body of the speech proper.

Sometimes more than one question is pertinent, and sometimes there are several possible answers to a single question. In such cases the problem is to choose which subheads you need to develop for the understanding of your audience, or which ones are most necessary to your purpose, or perhaps which ones you feel you can best handle in the time you have. In other words, the thesis states the topic and purpose. Once it is set, you ask it questions, using the answers to develop the body of the speech itself.

You will probably end up with from three to five subheads. Although the human mind *can* retain as many as fourteen to twenty different things in order, it does not want to. Three subdivisions in your speech would seem to make an almost ideal number. More than five will be too many unless you cannot help yourself.

On a slip of paper write your thesis, and under it jot down your subheads. If necessary, you could speak at length from no more outline than this. If called upon impromptu to speak upon a topic you know well, you can usually create such a thesis pattern as you go along—filling in with examples and illustrations from your ready knowledge and experience. The beauty of the method is that you cannot wander; you must of necessity be clear.

Two common organizational forms

Basically, any explanation can be thought of as being organized in one of two ways. The second is actually the reverse of the first, so they are easy to use and to remember. Both depend for their existence upon the thesis pattern.

Commonest of these is the didactic order, which uses the thesis pattern exactly as it is. Because audiences need to be awakened, now and then, to the basic thesis pattern we sometimes add some sort of an attention-getting introduction. Because audiences often need to be reminded of salient points, we frequently add a summation or conclusion.

The complete form of a didactically organized explanation, then, falls into the following simple order:

1. *Introduction:* some sort of an attention-getter, designed to lead the listener to the consideration of your main idea.

2. *Thesis statement:* a clear announcement of what you are to talk about, and some indication of what you plan to say about it.

3. *Body or development:* the explanation proper, with full detail, perhaps using visual aids, and so on.

4. *Conclusion:* a final restatement.

The first step arouses interest—a vital factor in good listening. The second step tells the listener what he is listening for, giving later developmental materials a sense of familiarity and helping the listener, as he listens, to spot central ideas. The third step presents the material, and the fourth step sums it up. When you use this pattern you actually present your main idea three times: in the thesis, in the body, and in the conclusion. As a result, even the erratic listener will in all probability catch at least your basic idea.

The thesis statement is the focus of the whole explanation. The main body of material supports or develops it; the conclusion restates it; and—if there is an introduction—this brief attention-getter leads directly into it. Therefore the speech should be thought out thesis statement first, rather than in the order of its presentation. Once you have your thesis pattern planned you can turn your attention to a possible introduction.

This form of organization—introduction, thesis, body, and conclusion—is so well known that it seems unnecessary to say anything more about it. Many teachers, however, know and teach this pattern for writing, yet fail to use it orally. As a result, their explanations are often rambling and incoherent, and they find themselves wondering why their pupils cannot seem to grasp what they are teaching. There is no better order for instructional speaking than the didactic order, and it should be used regularly.

Some teaching, however, grows out of an experience, and therefore cannot be didactically handled. This kind of an explanation turns the thesis pattern upon its head, letting the developmental materials lead into the thesis rather than grow out of it. Such a speech can be compared with one of Aesop's fables, in which he told the story first and then drew the moral. Similarly the teacher presents a demonstration first—or tells a story, or shows a film, or simply tosses the class into some kind of an experience without previous briefing. Then the class is shown how things add up to some sort of a generalized conclusion, which is actually the thesis.

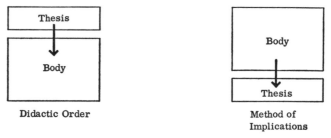

Fig. 8-2. The common organizational forms.

Thus, as we said in the beginning, there are two common organizational patterns for explanations. Commonest is the didactic order, but often used is a sort of reverse didactic pattern which we call the *method of implications*. Both depend completely upon the thesis pattern for their structure, and both use the thesis statement as a basic focal point. These patterns are structurally simple, offering ample opportunity for the speaker to use examples and visual aid materials for interest, and by their inherent "tightness" of form, they keep him on the track.

The student speaker

Whenever one of your pupils attempts to explain something, to influence the class, or to entertain his schoolmates, he is giving an informal speech. It is important that he learn to do these things well, yet it is also important that he not be made tense by too much adverse or detailed criticism. Learn to encourage him by accenting his strong points, while at the same time you tell him places where improvement could come about.

A good first step is to encourage especially the very young school children to develop the habit of using a thesis. "I saw a robin today!" one child may say, or "My daddy showed me how to fly a kite." After such a statement a natural development of points can easily follow.

Most of the talking done in the lower grades will use a time sequence, because the young child is action-minded and eager to tell what he did or what happened. A good teacher will help his pupils learn to keep things straight. But in doing so, he will also watch that what he says stimulates rather than inhibits the desire to speak and to listen.

As the child grows older he can be given more complicated oral assignments, such as reports and even debates or panel discussions. In every case, the same basic rule applies: use a thesis and stick to it.

Summary

The relationship among the *subject, topic,* and *thesis* of a talk is close, and vital to effective exposition. The listener has a right to expect a well-organized presentation, and, by putting the thesis into the central position in speech composition, the speaker can provide it. Once the topic is drawn out of the subject and turned into a thesis, the speech is fairly begun. After the thesis, the body of the talk should be developed. Then and only then is the speaker ready to prepare an introduction and a conclusion.

About 2500 years ago, in Book III of his *Rhetoric*, Aristotle said, "A speech has two parts. You must state your case, and you must prove it." For the teacher in the classroom, whose primary job is to explain, to clarify, or to inform, the categorical statement of this authority from the classic age still holds firmly true.

STUDY QUESTIONS

1. Why is good organization important to a speaker?

2. Distinguish between the subject and the topic of a speech.

3. What is the relationship between the topic and the thesis of a speech?

4. In what sense may a given item be both a subject and a topic?

5. Distinguish between a literal and an adapted thesis.

6. How is a thesis pattern developed from a thesis statement?

7. Why should the body of a talk be limited to from three to five subheads?

8. What are the parts of a didactic speech outline; what is the function of each part?

9. What are the parts of a talk organized according to the method of implications?

10. What is the main thing to encourage in children when they give informal talks?

SUGGESTED CLASS ACTIVITIES

1. If you wish to learn to give speeches, there is no substitute for giving one. Prepare a three to five minute expository talk suitable for teaching something. Identify your class first and ask the audience to imagine themselves as your students. The talk should be evaluated in terms of its depth of content, clarity of structure, interest, delivery.

2. Evaluate your class notes from your various professors in terms of their structure and general clarity. Prepare a short paper or talk on the thesis, "I want to explain why I feel that Professor _____ is my clearest lecturer this term."

SUPPLEMENTARY MATERIAL

McCall, Roy C., *Fundamentals of Speech,* New York: The Macmillan Company, 1949, Chapter II, "Subject-Topic-Thesis-Title," and Chapter III, "The Four-part Speech, Mainheads, and Example." This is an extremely clear presentation, brief and well-organized—directly to the point of this chapter.

Pronovost, Wilbert, *The Teaching of Speaking and Listening in the Elementary School,* New York: Longmans, Green and Co., 1959, Chapter II, "Talks." A detailed chapter, filled with case studies designed to give specific goals and procedures for classroom use. Notice especially the way in which he stresses the teacher's obligation to teach his pupils how to stick with a thesis!

Soper, Paul, *Basic Public Speaking,* 2nd ed., New York: Oxford University Press, 1956, Chapter V, "Outlining the Speech." If you translate Soper's "Statement of Specific Purpose" into what we (with McCall) have called the "thesis," there will be no confusion. This is a helpful, clear treatment—especially of the introduction.

9

Demonstrations

As speakers we often feel that we are the center of attention. Psychologists tell us, however, that such is rarely the case. When we speak, we simply provide one stimulus among the many striving for the listener's attention at any given instant. If the stimulus of our presentation is *stronger* than the others with which we are competing, or more *active*, or more *familiar*, or *better organized*, we will gain the listener's attention. But even this success, of course, is not the end of the battle, for there are limits to the attention span. Thus the speaker must continually work to hold his listener's attention, as well as to gain it.

The teacher who is talking all day to his audience must be especially conscious of attention because of its relationship to interest. Many years ago the psychologist, William James, taught us that what we pay attention to, we may well develop an interest in. A strong obligation, then, is placed upon the teacher, for attention, interest, and learning seem clearly to be related.

But, consider the teacher's problem. To give strength, activity, or an added sense of familiarity or pattern to all kinds of content material, hour after hour during the teaching day, will obviously require the fullest use of his every resource: his voice, his gestures and bodily action, his words and his content materials. The demonstration talk, with visual aids, can be a real help in the solution of his problem. The demonstration has built-in *action*. Because of the use of visual aid materials, there is also an immediate feeling of *familiarity*. The use of the visual material automatically gives a sense of *sequence and order* to the whole presentation, while the impact of both sight and sound adds *strength*. The demonstration, in other words, has inherent attention value.

But even this reason is not the only one for using a demonstration whenever possible. In addition to the interest value of high attention, there is also a learning value. Experiments show clearly that material which is learned through the eyes and ears *both* is learned more accurately, understood more clearly, and remembered longer than is material learned through the eyes alone (as in reading), or through the ears alone (as in a lecture).* You can probably still recall certain visual aids which were used by teachers you had years ago—perhaps a high school laboratory experiment, or a field trip in the fourth grade, or the way you reinforced your learning of certain words by sight from picture flash-cards, etc.

Demonstrations, in other words, are important parts of good teaching, both because of the short-range values of attention-interest, and because of the long-range values of attention-learning.

Planning the demonstration speech

The demonstration talk is basically a time sequence. Instead of being a narrative, however—as is the case in story-telling—the time

---

* See Walter S. Monroe, ed., *The Encyclopedia of Educational Research* (New York: The Macmillan Company, 1950), "Audio-Visual Materials." See also Edward J. J. Kramar and Thomas R. Lewis, "Comparison of Visual and Non-Visual Listening," *Journal of Communications*, Vol. I, No. 1 (Nov., 1951), pp. 16-20.

sequence appropriate to a demonstration involves the steps in a process.

As is true of any time sequence, the basic consideration is one of order, for the steps must be presented chronologically or the whole understanding of the listener will fail. Just what chronology is involved in a specific demonstration, of course, will be dictated by the nature of the process itself. Sometimes the steps are so many and so involved that even the use of visual aid materials cannot make the whole process clear. In such a case, the teacher must arbitrarily group steps under headings, and deal with them one group at a time. After stating his thesis for the whole talk, he then states a sub-thesis, develops the two or three steps pertinent to it, summarizes, states the next sub-thesis, and so on. This repeated process of statement-explanation-restatement will keep the listener clearly aware of what is occurring.

Almost invariably the over-all pattern for a demonstration talk should be didactic. In fact, even if the demonstration is only one part of what you plan to do, it is wise to treat this segment—no matter how brief—as a didactic unit. The advance warning of the thesis adds to the *listening readiness* of the hearer, hence to his ability to take in what you have to say. He is less likely to be confused by what he sees and hears, and more likely to subordinate irrelevancies if he knows your goal.

The plan of the demonstration speech, then, is essentially like the plan of any other expository talk. Because of the additional clarity it gives, the didactic order should be used, with the steps in the body of the speech being arranged in chronological order.

Kinds of visual aids, and problems in their use

Visual aids may be complete in themselves, as in the case of a sound motion-picture film—or they may serve as supplements to what is inherently an oral presentation. They are usually used in the classroom to interest or to clarify.

There are a number of ways to classify visual aids which are suitable for use in a demonstration, such as grouping them in accordance with their purpose in the speech or in terms of whether or not they *are* complete within themselves. The clearest way, however, is to think of visual aids under three main headings which are based upon the type of aid itself, rather than upon its use. We might call these three classes of visual materials the *real*, the *representational*, and the *personal*.

When a student demonstrates how to play a trombone and uses a real trombone to help him put the steps across, he is using *real* visual materials. If he uses charts or diagrams, or a film or slides, or if he draws on the blackboard, he is using *representational* visual materials. If, on the other hand, he merely shows us by his actions how a trombone works, he is using *personal* visual material. Each kind of visual material has its own special problems for the user, but all can help him be a better communicator if he uses them well.

Using the actual object or a full-scale model may be superior to some sort of a chart or diagram, or it may not be. Sometimes, for example, the actual object will be too complicated for your purpose—and it may not be easily and quickly broken down and reassembled. Sometimes it will be so large or so small that its size will necessitate the use of a chart instead. If, however, the object is suitable, available, and easily workable, by all means use it.

Representational materials are the most imaginative and varied of the visual aids. Flannelboards, slides, films, maps, charts, diagrams, pictures, blackboard drawings, cut outs, flip cards, strip charts, tear sheets—these are but a few of the many kinds which can be used. In the classroom, commonest of course are blackboard drawings. The "chalk-talk" technique is especially useful when you want to show changes in the drawing as you are talking. The sketch need not be good in the artistic sense, but it should be large enough to be seen easily. Keep the drawing as simple as possible. If it must be complicated, draw it ahead of time and cover it somehow until you are ready to use it.

Charts, maps, pictures, and the like follow the same general rules as the blackboard drawing so far as the degree of complexity is concerned. They, too, should be simple, large enough to be seen easily, and kept covered until needed. If you are using films, slides, or an opaque projector, check your equipment ahead of time, and be sure you can darken the room enough to use your materials. It pays to check your voltage, to have a spare projection bulb, and to be sure your cords and extensions are long enough. Representational materials are helpful, but they are subject to certain possibilities of error which must not be overlooked.

If you are using a personal demonstration, you should first of all be sure that what you plan can actually be done. For example, is the floor really clean enough to demonstrate the kind of artificial respiration which was formerly so universally taught? If a tap-dance step is to be demonstrated, what will it sound like in the room below you? Will there be room enough to demonstrate setting-up exercises with the group participating as a whole? You must be sure, in other words, that it is possible (and, for that matter, desirable!) to put on the demonstration at all. You must also be sure that everyone can see what you are doing, and that you can perform it clearly enough and with enough skill to be effective.

Whether real, representational, or personal materials should be used cannot be generalized. Your choice must depend upon your topic, upon your own creativity, and upon what is available for your use. Suit your visuals to your ideas, not *vice versa*.

Delivering the demonstration speech

A few general principles concerning the use of visual aids during a demonstration talk will bear special remembering.

First of all, your essential purpose in giving the demonstration must not be lost sight of: that purpose is to inform or explain. If the visual aid does not really contribute to understanding, *do not use it!* It should be clear, easy to see and grasp, simple and unified in its impact. In spite of the fact that visual aids *can* be used just for interest, in the classroom they probably should not be used for their own sake except on very rare occasions. If they can in any way help you make a point, however, use them.

Second, you must be sure that you never permit a visual aid to compete with you for attention. Get your speech underway before you turn to your aid or hold it; do not reveal your material until you are ready for it. Do not pass things around, because they are bound to interrupt your own speaking as they move up and down rows. You cannot wait for them, but must go on talking—sometimes, even, about something else entirely. The point is one of timing. If the visual aid is a good one, it will have strong attention value, and there is no use competing with it. If you introduce it at the precise moment it is needed, however, this strong attention-power is integrated into your total speech, and does not operate as a distraction from your goals.

Third, remember that the visual aid is not the speech. In fact, if you give a talk without any visual aids, most of your listeners will not miss them. If an unneeded visual aid is used, however, it will often operate as an irritating annoyance. As a rule, then, one or two major uses of visual aids in a talk will be sufficient. Too many can be worse than too few. Visual aids have something of the "gimmick" about them, and it is quite possible to seem to exploit your audience by overuse of visual attention devices. It helps keep sensible perspective to remember the true import of the term, visual *aid*, itself.

When you plan a demonstration, be sure to practice with your visual materials ahead of time. Television announcers live in horror of the oven door that will not open, or the aerosol bomb that jams. In the classroom, an upside-down slide or a film wound backwards can be just as disconcerting. Rule number one should be: be sure everything works, and that you can work it!

Be sure, also, that the materials are prepared in such a way that you can keep talking during the demonstration. When you stop talking to draw, or to adjust something, you run the risk of breaking rapport with your audience. Be careful, too, that you can talk to your listeners, and not just to your visual aid! Avoid long spells of not looking at your audience while you work. Stand to one side so your listeners can see what you are doing. If you are using the blackboard, write and draw with broad, heavy strokes. Keep your listeners in mind every minute. They are the ones who must see the material, and they obviously cannot see it through you!

The tips given in previous chapters concerning the time sequence and the didactic order should be enforced by you in your classroom during the speaking of all of your students whenever they give demonstrations. Their planning should be methodical, and their thesis clear. There is an increased joy of sharing for the little child when he can hold something, work it, point to it, draw it, or act it out. The circular pattern of speaker-listener-speaker interaction has a way of being surer when both the eyes and ears are involved. The little child, however, is likely to want to show his materials as a whole, rather than to take up any details. As a teacher you can help him by encouraging his efforts and clarifying them. In order to accomplish these ends, you may sometimes need to raise leading questions, such as, "And what is this for?" With experience, however, even your very young pupils will learn to give good demonstration talks.

With older students, the temptation tends to be the opposite of what it is with the younger ones—to bog down in details rather than to eliminate or forget them. Here your suggestions will probably center about the grouping of ideas, and the actual physical poise of the demonstrator—his clarity and his general quality of interest.

Summary

The demonstration is a time sequence with visual materials. It should be handled didactically, as a rule, with special attention to the chronology of the steps-in-a-process involved. The use of visual aids increases the attention of the listener, thereby adding to the interest of the talk, and fixing more surely listener comprehension. It is not an idle coincidence that we say, "I see," when we mean, "I understand." The demonstration is a ready tool for the good teacher, and a tool which will add easily to his effectiveness.

STUDY QUESTIONS

1. Why is a demonstration speech more attention compelling than a talk not using visual materials?

2. What are the four characteristics of a dominant stimulus?

3. Why does the teacher strive for attention?

4. What basic sequence or order does a demonstration talk follow? Why?

5. Why should a demonstration probably be outlined in accordance with the didactic method?

6. What are the three kinds of visual aid materials?

7. When should a chart or diagram be used instead of the actual object?

8. What are some general rules for effective use of the blackboard?

9. Why should you avoid calling attention to your visual aid until you are ready for it?

10. Why should you avoid passing materials around the audience during your talk?

SUGGESTED CLASS ACTIVITIES

1. Prepare an explanation of something in which you both demonstrate the object or mechanism, *and* use diagrams to clarify some part of the process. Practice it carefully so you can manage all the visuals easily and effectively. Keep talking!

2. Teach the class how to play some game. Have them actually *do* whatever is involved. You may want to use the board, and you will undoubtedly act out some of what you want them to do. Keep your instructions brief and clear, and watch what the class does to be sure they understand.

SUPPLEMENTARY READINGS

Bryant, Donald C., and Karl R. Wallace, *Fundamentals of Public Speaking*, 2nd ed., New York: Appleton-Century-Crofts, Inc., 1953, Chapter 11, "Visual Materials." This chapter gives an especially good treatment of charts and graphs, and is followed by an extremely helpful bibliography.

Gray, Giles Wilkeson, and Waldo W. Braden, *Public Speaking: Principles and Practice*, New York: Harper & Bros., 1951, Chapter XII, "Visual Supports." Note especially the pictures in this and in the previous chapter; they show demonstration speeches being given and are well worthy of your serious attention.

10

Conferences with students and parents

As a rule, the conferences which teachers hold, whether with students or with parents, are concerned with specific problems. These conferences are almost without exception highly personal in their content and highly complex in their psychological implications. Unfortunately, most teachers have had very little real training in counselling and guidance. Yet they are expected to perform in these areas in a specialized manner, achieving important results which may vitally affect their students' whole lives. It is important, therefore, that we consider conferences and the role which speech plays in them.

In Chapter 7 it was pointed out that there are only three kinds of statements which can be made about a thing: a descriptive or objective statement, a speculative statement, or a judgmental statement. It is crucial in the conference to keep these kinds of statements clearly separated. Judgments should be based on facts, and speculations should be recognized for what they really are. If the conference is to have any success at all, that success is clearly dependent upon the verbalized interpersonal relationship which develops. What we say to one another obviously affects our success in achieving our goals.

There should be a striving together for common understanding and a sense of common purpose. Areas of disagreement should be narrowed down by the search for common grounds for agreement, and by the effort to isolate and identify the real problem. There should be a minimum of quibbling and bickering, and there should, of course, never be any name-calling or use of sarcasm. These things are all dependent upon your checking, constantly and carefully, the kinds of statements which you make. Lack of training, however, makes teachers all too often blind to the importance of clearly separating their judgments and their speculations from their facts. An awareness of the full implications of our statements and great care in all verbalizing of thoughts and feelings can do much to help a teacher do an effective job as an advisor.

The conversational basis of conferences

The conference with a pupil or a parent is, first of all, a purposive conversation. This concept, however, is not the whole picture, for there is also a built-in status relationship. Obviously you must be very sure of your own role if the conference is to be worthwhile. You must constantly be the teacher, and you must be very careful not to exploit, or default your role.

If you exploit your role too far, your "authority" is likely to act as a conversation-stopper for your students. I am sure you have known teachers who were unapproachable because their authority status was so unbending. Similarly, with parents, an overly apparent feeling of status on the part of the teacher is likely to result in irritation and annoyance. The parent will recognize your rights of authority over his child, but if you stress them, he may well become angry.

On the other hand, if you completely default your role as a teacher you are likely to lose the respect of your students. From you they want friendly, understanding leadership—not necessarily another pal. Parents will react more warmly, perhaps, to your efforts to talk with them on their own ground, but they, too, will not forget your role even if you do. They expect you to be the expert you are trained to be, and they will want to learn from you—to find out answers.

The conversation of a teacher-student conference, despite the rather clear built-in status relationship and despite the urgent sense of goal, must be an honest effort at free interaction. The same thing is true of the teacher-parent conference. In the basic definition, then, they are alike—both are, to repeat, purposive conversations with a built-in status relationship. The difference lies in the role you, the teacher, will play, rather than in your purpose or the basic technique of handling the conference.

Modern psychology views man as a whole organism, operating within a total field or frame of reference. As we have pointed out many times already, behavior is caused and can, therefore, be changed. In a conference you can get at causes of behavior in a way that may help you bring about important and desirable changes.

Here you can find out, if you are sincerely friendly, what is really bothering your pupils. You will not do it, however, by the direct question technique, and neither will you usually be able to do it in a fifteen minute conference held during the first week of school. Successful counselling takes time and a mutual development and understanding of your interacting roles as pupil and teacher—a building up of mutual trust and acceptance.

One of the most effective means of drawing a person out during a conference is to use the method of reflected feelings. This approach to counselling is especially useful if the problem is one of a personal or disciplinary nature. Suppose you have a pupil who is tense with feelings of aggression toward you and the class. You will accomplish nothing by inhibiting him even further—to do this will obviously only increase his tensions. But you can, through a conference, explore how he really feels about himself and you. As you listen to him, put yourself in his shoes. Maybe his hostility is an honest reaction to the distorted world he sees—can you help him get a new perspective without just "pulling your rank" and thereby confirming all his feelings and fears? Maybe something has been done or said which he has interpreted out of context. Can you fill in the missing pieces? As you do so, be sure to reinforce his own sense of worth by restating what he has said. "I guess that did seem rather unfair, didn't it?" you might say, or "You were really upset about that, weren't you?" Thus encouraged, he will be more likely to spill out the real causes of his complaints. Be careful not to seize the conversation yourself, but play the role of sympathetic listener, offering occasional comments. Even if you are not trained to do counselling, you can in this way gain information which will be useful to the counsellors in your school and will provide helpful insight for yourself.

If the conference is of a problem-solving kind centering on the mastery of some task, the same general technique can be helpful to bring out the real areas of misunderstanding.

People converse, of course, for a wide variety of reasons—and, during a conference, several of these may be in the picture. For example, a good bit of the conversation will probably be self-exploratory; some of it will be an effort to understand one another; some to release tension. Some even may be pure exhibitionism. Even this list is incomplete. The point is that conversation will by definition be rather hard to channel. Conversation, in other words, depends for its existence upon a free flow of ideas.

In your effort to give design to the conversation in a conference you should strive, first of all, for some common ground. This will require each of you to look outward from your own sheltered selves and to strive consciously and deliberately to be more "you-centered" and less "me-centered" in your topics and language.

Do not be afraid of the trivial. After all, it is a rather poor sort of neighbor who will not have some interest in your reactions to weather, family, prices, and the like! But do try to channel your end of the interchange so that your questions will necessitate more than yes-or-no answers. "Cold today, isn't it?" is actually a conversation-stopper rather than a conversation-starter. The reply, "Yeah, sure is!" comes, and that is that! "I haven't seen the paper yet. What does it say about the weather?" is much more likely to start things going.

When you ask a question—which is, incidentally, always a good way to start a conversation—you are really calling on the other person for something. It may be you ask for information or for his opinion, or maybe you are seeking his best judgment or advice. To be thus sought after is in itself complimentary; it creates an atmosphere favorable to good conversation.

In a conference, then, try to make your conversation "you-centered"; search for common grounds of interest and agreement; do not be afraid to spend some time in discussing the seemingly trivial; and ask *leading* questions. These things will be easier to do if your own role in the conversation is clear to you and if your goals have been fixed.

The structure of a conference

Conferences are of two basic types: the conference to resolve a problem, and the informational conference. In general, the overall pattern of each can be thought of in terms of three main characteristics: stability, flexibility, and collaboration. The conference achieves stability of purpose by a mutual effort on the part of those conferring to limit the field of consideration and to fix its goals. Flexibility is assured when the atmosphere or climate of the conference itself includes a sense of mutual trust and mutual interest. Collaboration occurs when the conversationalists avoid the debate format, choosing, instead, to search out means of working together.

The conference on a *problem* commences by a statement of the problem itself. There needs to be a certain amount of verbal exploring to insure that all the conferees are actually talking about the same things. Once this point of stability concerning the problem has been reached, there should be a movement into the consideration of goals, then the evaluation of possible solutions.

The *informational* conference begins with an explanation which is followed by the opportunity to ask questions. Experiments have shown conclusively that the ability to question freely helps to insure comprehension. Listeners who could question gained much clearer understanding of information and instructions than listeners who could not.* Take time, therefore, to answer all questions, and to answer them with an impression of sincere acceptance. Otherwise some important detail may well be lost.

Do not go into a conference unprepared. Think, first of all, of what you hope to accomplish. What is your real goal? What subsidiary goals have you in mind? Perhaps you hope to find out something, or to help some child master a problem skill, or simply to report to a parent on his child's progress. Write your purpose down, and then think what else is involved. In finding out what you need to know, you may want to build a better feeling between yourself and your student. In teaching the skill, you may hope also to instill more confidence in the learner. In reporting progress to a parent, you may also hope to build good public relations for your school—or even to gain a new P.T.A. member. Not until you have all of your goals clearly in mind are you ready to prepare specifically for your conference.

The second step is to organize all the things you will need to carry out the conference and to have them handy. You should have books and materials ready to use if you plan to help a child with a learning problem. If you are holding a progress-report conference with a parent, you should have the report, as well as other pertinent records, where you can see it and refer to it. As a part of your organizing, you may wish to jot down the main points you want to cover, in order that you do not forget any when the conference is actually begun.

If the conference is a problem-solving one, your specific preparations may have to be a bit more detailed. You will want to apply

* See Harold J. Leavitt and Ronald A. H. Mueller, "Interaction and Equilibrium," in A. Paul Hare, Edgar F. Borgatta and Robert F. Bales, *Small Groups: Studies in Social Interaction* (New York: Alfred A. Knopf, 1955), p. 414 ff.

the steps in the reflective thinking process. Since the situation is essentially conversational, a detailed outline would be out of place, but a short list of leading questions you feel should be covered would be quite in order. These questions must be arranged in a definite sequence if sensible interaction is to result.

1. *What is the problem?* Here you will want to know such things as: What is the present situation? How did this set of conditions develop? What has already been done to change things? Where have these efforts at improvement succeeded and failed? Why? Where do we seem to be going now? Where should we be going? and so on.

2. *What can be done?* Here you will ask: Can things be left alone to take their course? Can minor adjustments be made which will improve things or must we start over with a new approach? What would be the advantages, or disadvantages, of each of these alternative courses of action? And so on.

3. *What solution can we agree upon?*

4. *How can we put it into effect?*

These last two points, of course, cannot be anticipated, but will grow out of the conference itself. It may well be that more than one meeting will have to be held before you can actually work out a solution.

Once your conference goals are clearly set, your materials gathered and ready for use, and your general scheme for the conversation drawn up, you are ready for the conference itself. This advance thought will stabilize and direct the conference along channels which will yield results.

Be careful, however, not to be too patriotic about your preparations. You can stifle the conference in your effort to keep things moving along according to your plan. After all, you cannot successfully be reflecting feelings and acting the autocrat at the same moment! When forced to choose between your agenda and your goal, the goal is obviously the more important. In addition to stability, then, there must also be the flexible give-and-take of easy, free conversation. Unless both stability and flexibility are inherent in the situation itself, collaboration will be impossible.

Without collaboration, the conference will not only fail to achieve its goal, it will be a complete waste of time.

There are three steps you must go through prior to a conference: set your goals, get your materials ready for use, and plan an agenda covering all points that you feel must be covered. When you have completed these steps, consider various possible ways the conversation might go, preparing yourself to adjust to whatever may occur.

Try to avoid taking notes during the conference in order to keep your personal interaction as free as possible. Once the conference is over, allow yourself time to write down whatever needs to be recorded. Because of that built-in status relationship, watching your pencil record all that is said will be likely to shut off free conversation by pupil *or* parent! You can remember what you need to write down until the conference is over.

Summary

The students in your classes will welcome the feeling that they can come to you with problems. Probably the nicest compliment any student can pay any teacher is to give him trust and confidence. Call for conferences as often as you sensibly can, for they can give insight into causes of behavior which can never be gained from classroom contact. Keep your facts, your speculative guesses, and your judgments separated from one another, and keep your own role in the conference clearly in mind. Use the technique of reflecting feelings to build an atmosphere of freedom and mutual trust, and try to seek for common areas of interest, common concepts of the problem at hand, and common understanding. Use leading questions, and keep the conference structured in terms of its goal: the solving of a problem, or the sharing of information.

Almost any intelligent, well-organized human being can find a way to manage a classroom and keep things going somehow. The true art of teaching, however, is found in making the classroom a place where learning is eagerly sought, where human values are warmly respected, and where goals are constantly changing and widening.

STUDY QUESTIONS

1. Why is it especially important in a conference to keep clearly separated and labelled the three kinds of statements which can be made about a thing?

2. Define the relationship between conversation and a teacher-pupil or teacher-parent conference.

3. What is the role of the teacher in a teacher-pupil conference? In a teacher-parent conference?

4. What is the purpose of such conferences? Why are they important?

5. Name and explain several reasons why people converse. Do they all apply to teacher-pupil and teacher-parent conferences?

6. What is meant by "establishing common ground"?

7. What are the two kinds of conferences discussed in the chapter?

8. How is the problem-solving conference organized?

9. How is the informational conference organized?

10. What steps should you go through prior to a conference?

SUGGESTED CLASS ACTIVITIES

1. Prepare a brief paper outlining a problem which you, as a teacher, might wish to discuss in a conference with a pupil. You will wish to explain exactly what the problem is and to consider just when the conference might best be held. What are your goals? What materials will you need at hand? What points will you need to cover? Divide the class up into pairs. With a classmate, you can role-play your conference. Let your partner read your paper silently first, then let him ask you any questions he may have. Then begin. You will have no audience, for the others in the class will be doing the same thing. When you have finished, talk with your partner about what you did—where it went well, and where it did not. After you have read your partner's paper and played out his situation, you can finish your papers by showing the strengths and weaknesses of your plans: where you feel you might succeed in a real situation, and where you feel you might not—and why.

2. Do the same thing for a teacher-parent situation if you have time.

SUPPLEMENTARY MATERIAL

Brown, Charles T., *Introduction to Speech*, Boston: Houghton Mifflin Company, 1955, Chapter 11, "Conversation." These are interesting and thoughtful pages, mainly at the pragmatic level of what to do and why, in order to be a good conversationalist.

Sondel, Bess, *Are You Telling Them?* Englewood Cliffs, N. J.: Prentice-Hall, Inc., 1947, Chapter VI, "Conversation Goes to Work." Miss Sondel is herself a highly conversational writer. Do not let your interest in her examples lead you to overlook the real meat of what she says. So far as I know, this chapter says what we know about the matter with more insight than any. Stability, flexibility, and collaboration are treated in detail.

The Staff of the Division on Child Development and Teaching Personnel, *Helping Teachers Understand Children*, Washington, D.C.: American Council on Education, 1945, pp. 3-8. This is a moving report on an experimental study of a school system. In these few pages are many examples of the misuse of statements which are judgmental. Read it to see why we have so stressed the importance of the kinds of statements you make about a thing.

11

Class discussion

Class discussion is one of the most important parts of teaching. In many ways it has more far-reaching effects than any lecture or demonstration the teacher may give and has more influence than any textbook assignment.

Experimental evidence seems to indicate that materials are learned better through discussion than through the straight lecture.* They are learned better, first of all, in the sense that they are learned more accurately. When the student is free to raise questions, he can check his listening, can range out more freely from theory to application, and can correct errors in his understanding

* See Walter S. Monroe, ed., *The Encyclopedia of Educational Research* (New York: The Macmillan Company, 1950), "Methods of Teaching." See also Harold W. Bernard, *Psychology of Learning and Teaching* (New York, McGraw-Hill Book Company, Inc., 1954), Chapter 5, "Factors Which Facilitate Learning."

which might go unnoticed in the lecture situation. Materials are also learned better, in the sense that they are more likely to be retained. When a student listens, he is operating largely at the level of perception. What conscious evaluations he makes are of the order of "preparations for" something—some application, some comment, some question, which is to come later. When he engages in discussion, however, his evaluations are immediate, and usually lead to other evaluations as well. Thus the time lag between perception and application is shortened, and the total learning impression is, consequently, strengthened.

We also know that discussion operates at a level of *human feelings* which is important. Not only does discussion have its effect upon what people learn, but it has an effect upon how they *feel* about learning. If a person participates in a thing personally, he gives—he shares. The thing becomes his. In discussion, moreover, he can even excell—he can be the one to whom others look for comments and ideas. He can belong, he can be of importance, he can, in other words, salve his own ego and find satisfactions in what he does, developing his ability to make interpersonal adjustments, and learning new self-confidence.

A good teacher is, without exception, a good discussion leader. Friendly, conscious interaction between student and teacher cannot be overrated. Where it does not exist, the classroom becomes a jungle. Students bait the teacher, or worse, the teacher baits the students, sometimes to the point of violence. The result is either chaos or else iron discipline. In order to avoid the one extreme, however, it is not necessary to adopt the other. The thought of row after row of silent, cowed children, with their frightened hands folded is a chilling one—yet there are still elementary classrooms where this sort of thing exists. Of course discipline is necessary, but it must be based on mutual respect rather than upon fear, indifference, or hatred. Mutual respect can only come when there is a chance for two-way communication to take place.

Class discussion, then, can aid in the pupils' learning and in their own personality development. It can also serve as the touchstone of good class spirit. But it can only do these things when it is well managed.

The role of class discussion

There is some profit in considering what good class discussion is not. In the first place, it is not simply class recitation in which the teacher plays inquisitor and the pupil plays quiz contestant striving for the prize of a high grade. This sort of thing is the very antithesis of good class discussion—the student talks only to the teacher, and only on the grounds the teacher lays down. The obvious result will be a general feeling that nothing matters except oneself and whether one's own answers can get by. If any feeling of relatedness is built at all among the students, it will be competitive. The student soon begins to low-rate certain of his classmates, fear or envy others, and to try to figure out his own self-defense. In such a classroom, cheating is inevitable and any hope of developing positive or social values might just as well be set aside. The teacher is playing the role of "top sergeant" in true stereotype form, and the students will quickly learn to "gold-brick" their way through. Why not? They obviously have no responsibility to one another—only to themselves.

Good class discussion, on the other hand, is not just general noise and confusion, either. Any kind of group discussion implies, first of all, that a group exists. Classroom anarchy is not likely to result in any feeling of "group"! After all, a group has common goals, identified in common and sought in common. Group discussion of any kind is, in its essence, an orderly process based upon mutual respect.

The role of discussion in the classroom is to aid the group to set goals and realize them, not to turn the classroom into a verbal shambles. This role cannot be realized until certain prior conditions are met. There must be an atmosphere of acceptance in the classroom. As a teacher, you must accept the fact that students can teach one another, and that in some cases they have a right to set their own limits on what is interesting, or valuable, or proper. You will tend to get what you expect from your students. If you expect them to be stupid, time-wasting, irresponsible juveniles, they will probably not bother much to change your concept—only to stay out of your way. If, however, you expect them to show intelligence and responsibility, they generally will do so.

In addition to this attitude of acceptance in the classroom, there must also be some real preparation for the discussion itself—both by the teacher and by the students. Class discussion *can* be merely sound and fury, of course; but when the facts are known to the participants, and when the leader has planned with care, the results can also be excellent. Except in terms of setting up goals, class discussion should probably not be attempted without allowing time for careful previous preparation.

If the class is well prepared, and the proper feeling of "group" exists, a third requisite to good class discussion must be considered: objectivity. Of course it is hard to be shown wrong, but students and teachers must both learn not to expect perfection in themselves. If the teacher "manipulates" the discussion, it will not long continue in any profitable sense. If the students use the discussion as a way to trick and trap one another or the teacher, again nothing profitable will come of it. A good class discussion will divorce personalities and ideas and will be concerned with the attempt to develop group understanding, group agreement on an issue, or a group solution to a problem.

Acceptance, information, objectivity—these three, plus a scientific approach, will yield good results. Class discussion, like any other group activity, must have a consensus about goals and methods if it is to be successful. As in the case of the problem-solving conference, the reflective thinking pattern with some variation is in order: 1) define and analyze the present situation, 2) determine your goals, 3) consider possible solutions, 4) reach some conclusion, and 5) plan for the action you will take. If you will follow these tested steps, your discussion will be orderly and, therefore, more likely to be profitable and interesting.

Kinds of class discussion

If the problem is one of policy, the steps in the reflective thinking pattern should be followed exactly. Policy questions are concerned with what should be done, and might involve such classroom considerations as: How can a class project be organized? Should the class plan a field trip? How can school safety be improved? And so on. Often classes are organized into clubs. When they are, most of their discussions are at the level of policy. All classes consider policy matters from time to time, although less frequently, perhaps, than other kinds of problems.

For example, many class discussions dealing with lessons concern questions of fact and questions of belief or value rather than questions of policy. Common questions of fact include such matters as: What is the author's point of view? What are the causes or effects, of such-and-such? What is the nature of so-and-so? And so on. Common questions of belief or value deal with: What is important? What is useful or effective? What would be of benefit? Such questions follow the reflective thinking pattern only up to a point. Obviously no *solution* as such is called for. The problem must be defined clearly, however, and analysis must precede any conclusion which is ultimately agreed upon. The pattern, in other words, would be to define the question itself, analyze the possible answers, and state and justify your conclusion. The difficulty is to get students to give enough time to the first two of these three and to keep them from rushing headlong into the third step. Commonly raised questions—What do we know about this? How do we know it? Of what use is knowing it?—all too often go unanswered, or even unconsidered.

Sometimes the teacher serves as chairman, and sometimes not, depending on the topic. Even primary school children can serve as moderators, however. For example, a third grader can guide his classmates in reviewing safety rules. To help things, if necessary, the teacher might ask one child to explain the rules, and let the others add to the explanation. Or she might even turn the whole thing into a game by asking one child to "play like" he was a new student and to find out about school safety from his classmates. Older children can be given a question and put into small conversation groups of six or eight to work out a group answer and report back to the class as a whole. Or the teacher might set up a system in which he tossed out a question, asking everyone who knew anything about it to hold his hand up and keep it up so long as he still had something to say. In this way students begin to interact, for they must now add to and/or correct things said by others in the class. In any case, the basic questions remain about the same in their intent to discover what is known, how it can be verified, and how it can be used.

The class discussion aimed at the definition and resolution of group problems is equally subject to several means of handling. Probably one of the commonest is the use of parliamentary procedure. Sometimes the class is even organized with officers and by-laws; at other times the structure itself is more informal, although the main principles of action remain the same. Speakers seek recognition, a formal motion is made, a vote is taken, and so on. Almost as common is the working committee technique, in which various projects are assigned to specific groups who must work them out together. Whether the teacher guides the discussion, or an elected or informally chosen leader does; whether or not parliamentary procedure is used; and whether the group is an action committee or the whole class, the same steps will apply: problem, goal, possible solutions, solution, and plan for action.

Pointers for the leader and the participants

The principal thing for the leader to keep in mind is that he wants the group to talk. This seemingly simple fact, however, implies a good bit about what the leader will do.

For example, he must plan exactly how he will get the conversational ball rolling. There are only about three possibilities open to him: he can ask a direct question of a person or of the group; he can raise a "leading question" designed to stimulate controversy; or he can use a case study approach. Each of these ways of beginning the conversation is worthy of some consideration, as well as what might logically follow.

The difficulty with the *direct question* technique is that it so easily leads to the recitation. The leader must be very careful that he does not simply hear an answer and evaluate it. There should be a minimum use of the phrases "that's right!" and "that's wrong!"

and a very frequent use of the questions, "What else might we say?" and "How do you feel about that?" Students should be encouraged to question one another so the conversation does not become a series of dialogs, all co-featuring the teacher. It often helps to get the chairs out of formal rows, and to sit down yourself as you lead the discussion. Always be careful to warn the student ahead of time that the question is for him, by starting with his name rather than ending with it. Otherwise you pounce on him, and he may be so startled that he will not be able to tell you what you really want and need to know. Ask more than one question, if you need to, to clarify a point, and do not hesitate to explain your question if it seems to be necessary. There is no magic in asking a thing in any one particular way! If you use the conversation group method, write the questions for each group on the blackboard. Five or six minutes to work out some sort of answer is usually enough. Be sure that no group is permitted to discuss more than one question at a time. The procedure is usually as follows: ask the question you wish discussed (write it on the blackboard); permit some time for free discussion in the small groups of six to eight; have each group report back to the whole class for discussion by everyone.

In the *leading question* method of stimulating discussion, the leader tosses a question to the group as a whole. Usually the question proper is preceded by some sort of introductory statement designed to stimulate interest. A frequently used technique is to set up pros and cons, and ask for group expressions of opinion. Another common technique is to state something erroneous, and ask what is wrong. These, however, are merely devices for commencing the conversation. Once it has begun, despite the size of the group, the leader proceeds much as he would with a panel discussion. This means that he tries to say as little as possible, drawing others out instead. He summarizes from time-to-time to indicate what has been covered, and—if the group is ready—he steers the conversation to the next phase of the consideration. He insists that the steps in the reflective thinking process be followed as far as the topic will allow. He tries to silence the talkative members, and to bring out the silent ones. The result, if well handled, is that the class conversation quickly becomes cross-directional, instead of everything being said to or through the leader. Once a class becomes accustomed to being expected to participate, this kind of learning can be exciting. Participants, however, must learn to hold their own in the conversation, at the same time giving others a chance to talk. They should learn to look at one another when they talk, and to appear interested and attentive while listening. Participants must be careful not to be too personal, and should avoid using the humorous jibe. They should talk one at a time, and learn to use the problem-solution method of reflective thinking themselves in order to help the leader in his efforts to keep things on the track.

The case study method offers another approach. This kind of discussion has been called *problem teaching,* because here the teacher often sketches in the details of some problem, asking the class to discuss how it might be met. An adaptation of this basic method is used for the teaching of principles; an illustration clearly demonstrating some tenet is told, and the class is asked some leading question concerning it. "What did you think of this?" is a frequently used query. Occasionally the case is role-played, then discussed—or presented on a film. It generally will be presented somehow in narrative form, and questions concerning the narrative proper are usually permitted before the discussion commences.

Once the discussion moves to a conclusion, regardless of its type, the leader must take over again in order to sum up.

Summary

What we learn consists, to a large extent, of related symbols, which we mainly acquire without ever having the opportunity to observe the realities they represent. Because it is difficult to learn abstractly, class discussion fills a vital need. It can provide involvement for the student, making his learning less abstract, more related to reality. In fact, the act of verbalizing itself seems to work to insure understanding and remembrance.

Good class discussion requires that the teacher set the stage from the first day of class in such a way that the students know that they have responsibilities. Within the classroom there must be a feeling of acceptance for student comments and ideas. Students must converse objectively from a basis of real information. The discussion should follow, as much as possible, the steps of the reflective thinking process. Permissive but stable leadership is called for, and the class members must be taught their responsibilities as participants. The cooperative consideration of a mutual problem, the sharing of information on a topic of common interest—these are highly desirable ends. The pooling of ignorance, however, and the exchange of insults, are undesirable, unnecessary, and uncalled for.

STUDY QUESTIONS

1. Why is group discussion an important classroom tool?
2. In what ways does group discussion differ from class recitation? From mere conversation?
3. What attitudes must be present in the classroom if effective class discussion is to take place?
4. What does a question of policy concern? What steps in the reflective thinking process apply in the discussion of a question of policy?
5. What does a question of belief or value concern? What steps in the reflective thinking process apply in the discussion of it?
6. What does a question of fact concern? What steps in the reflective thinking process apply in the discussion of it?
7. What is the job of the leader of a class discussion? Of the participants?
8. Give three ways in which the direct question technique can be used. How does it differ from the leading question technique?
9. What is the case study (problem teaching) method, and how does it work?
10. What is the relation of good evidence, facts, and general information, to group discussion? What is the relation of learning itself to group discussion?

SUGGESTED CLASS ACTIVITIES

1. During your next week of classes, analyze what happens when a class discussion is held. Gather specific data concerning:

   1) the kinds of questions which were discussed.
   2) the scope of participation—how many actually took part?
   3) the technique of beginning and ending the discussion.
   4) the way in which the reflective thinking process was or was not used.

Write up your data in a short paper, evaluating how good these discussions were. Speculate concerning why these discussions were or were not effective.

2. Prepare a beginning for a class discussion on some topic. Use the direct question, the leading question, or the case study method. Once class discussion has begun, sit down and let the next person try to get things going.

SUPPLEMENTARY MATERIAL

Backus, Ollie L., *Speech in Education,* New York: Longmans, Green and Company, 1943, pp. 245-248, "Class Discussion." A clear, usable, brief treatment which aptly summarizes what needs to be said.

Cantor, Nathaniel, *Dynamics of Learning,* Buffalo: Henry Stewart, Inc., 1956, Chapter 11, "The Activity of the Teacher." A fascinating chapter on how a good college teacher operates through class discussion.

Douglas, Harl R., *Modern Methods in High School Teaching,* Boston: Houghton Mifflin Company, 1926, Chapter VIII, "Socialized Class Procedure." An older book, but still extremely informative and useful. How frightening, how shocking that attacks leveled at educational methods so long ago would still ring so true!

Fessenden, Seth A., Roy Ivan Johnson, and P. Merville Larson, *The Teacher Speaks,* Englewood Cliffs, N. J., Prentice-Hall, Inc., 1954, pp. 136-152, "Class Discussion; Other Forms of Discussion." A clear, matter-of-fact presentation.

section three

Classroom speaking: the student's speech

It is grossly unfair to consider students in only three categories, and when we do so, we must bear in mind that those who rank high, low, and in the middle in speech ability are where they are for widely divergent reasons. There are a few at the very bottom and a few at the very top of the scale, however, who do need special consideration. It was because of their needs that these chapters were written.

The purposes of this section are to show you what you cannot do, and to suggest to you what you can do to help your students develop speaking skill. It has been said that a man must know both what he does know and what he does not know if he is to be wise. Read on, then, to acquire principles and a little insight rather than in the hope of detailed methodological instruction.

12

Aiding the speech handicapped

There are certain things a teacher can and should do to help the child in his class who has a serious speech problem of a clinical type. First of all, certainly, he should insist upon a medical examination. If possible, he should also insist upon referral to a trained speech clinician. In other words, the teacher's first job in such a case is to try to get qualified professional help for the child. When this help is available, and when the parents are willing to avail themselves of it, the teacher simply acts as an assistant, carrying out the instructions the specialists suggest.

No untrained person should attempt speech correction on his own. The consequences of what are sometimes well-intended efforts are all too often tragic. Every school system should have a trained speech therapist as a member of its staff if at all possible. If your school is too small or for any other reason does not hire such a person, you should write your closest university speech department and find out what services are available near you.

To insist upon such expert assistance, however, does not mean that you can do nothing to help the child with a speech handicap to develop more acceptable patterns of speech. Even when the child has the benefit of working with a capable therapist, much depends upon you. When there is no clinician in your school, even more depends upon you and what you do. It takes several years of specialized training to qualify as a speech therapist certified by the American Speech and Hearing Association. The few hours you will be able to give to the subject will not make you an expert, but they may put you in a better position to help those who are trained. Even more important, they may prevent you from doing the wrong things and causing severe, lasting, psychological or physical damage to some child entrusted to your care and guidance.

The nature of speech handicaps

There are no exact figures, but between one and five of every one hundred children seem to have speech so unclear that some sort of speech therapy is indicated. Sometimes, of course, there are organic causes for their speech problems, and the teacher should learn to recognize these cases and to understand their special peculiarities, even though they will not be common in his classes.

There is, for example, the *cleft palate*. As the infant develops in the womb, for some reason the hard palate does not grow completely together, leaving a hole or *cleft* between the cavity of the mouth and the cavity of the nose. Sometimes this cleft is so severe that the upper gum ridge and even the upper lip are also parted. This condition is called a *cleft lip*. It is possible to have a cleft palate without having a cleft lip, but it is not customary to have a cleft lip without having a cleft palate. When the cleft is so large that the soft palate does not grow over it and cover it up, many simple tasks such as swallowing and speaking become painfully difficult. Today, surgical repair is almost automatic; but often the strange, nasal, muffled *cleft palate speech* persists even after surgery. Such speech is in no way related to intellectual ability, and the child should certainly not be thought of as stupid because of it. Such speech can, however, if uncorrected, lead to serious personality maladjustments.

Another obvious cause of speech difficulty is *cerebral palsy.* This complex physical disorder is generally thought to be the result of brain injury, and is characterized by a lack of muscular coordination which is sometimes almost total. Again, the handicap is not universally related to intellectual ability and the child should not be automatically thought of as mentally deficient, although mental retardation among the cerebral palsied is more common than among people in general. Therapy is heart-breakingly slow, and the correction is rarely complete; but understandable speech and useful motor skill can be developed in some cases.

A third physical impairment which can result in defective speech is a *severe hearing loss.* The really deaf child will almost without exception be educated in the special residential schools of our various states. The hard-of-hearing child, however, will usually be enrolled in regular classes in our public schools. If your school has routine hearing checks, these tests will probably turn up those children who have a hearing loss. If not, however, the detection of the loss becomes *your* responsibility. Hearing impairment is especially important in speech because of the effect it can have upon the child's ability to learn how to produce words accurately. Sometimes delayed or retarded speech is the result.

In addition to cleft palate, cerebral palsy, and hearing impairment, speech may also be slow to develop, or defective in its development, because of a *general lack of intelligence.* In all of these cases, of course, expert medical counsel is needed, and the ordinary untrained layman can do little that is specific except to understand and to offer his friendship. You will probably have children in your classroom from time to time who have physical handicaps that affect their speech. When you do—and it will not be frequent—be *sure* to seek expert guidance and assistance.

Much more common than such organic speech problems, certainly, are the ones that have primarily psychological or behavioral causes. Among these speech problems, the most serious is *stuttering*. Others include the myriad of *articulatory problems*, centering about the production of specific sounds, such as *s*, *l*, and *r*; *voice problems* such as breathiness, hoarseness, and nasality. The teacher in the primary grades will also rather frequently have a pupil with delayed speech which is not traceable to any organic cause. With all these cases, as with the organic ones, the first step is to get expert guidance.

Authorities are not in complete agreement concerning the specific cause of stuttering, but they do agree upon two things of real importance to all classroom teachers: stuttering blocks become more frequent and more severe when the speaker feels anxiety, and stutterers cannot usually be identified even by experts until the stuttering pattern itself has become chronic and fairly severe.* In other words, unless a parent or a friend—or you, the teacher— told the speech correctionist that five-year-old Johnny was a stutterer, he probably would be unable to pick Johnny out from among the rest of his kindergarten playmates. When you make Johnny nervous about his speech, or call him a stutterer, you may very well be adding to the anxiety which is related to his problem, or even pinning on him the damaging label of stutterer when it is not justified. Stuttering, as a rule, has deep-seated psychological relationships, some of which may be causal. Expert clinical guidance is clearly called for.

When one of your students has continued hoarseness, or a husky, muffled voice quality which seems to be his usual way of speaking, by all means insist that a medical examination be made. It may be that you will want a psychiatric analysis as well. If nothing medical is wrong, encourage him to begin breathing exercises, and help him with vocal drills such as those suggested at the end of Chapter 1. Be sure first, however, that his problem *is* one of speech improvement rather than one of clinical implications.

* Wendell Johnson, ed., *Stuttering in Children and Adults* (Minneapolis: University of Minnesota Press, 1955), especially Chap. 3.

As was pointed out earlier, really serious vocal cases will not clear up without professional therapy.

The same things can be said concerning articulatory defects. A few improvement exercises are included at the end of Chapter 2. The *lisp*, the substitution of *w* for *l* and *r*, the distortion or omission of sounds and other such behavioral differences are, without question, the commonest of all speech defects. During the first four grades, maturation alone takes care of many of these problems, but after the age of eight, automatic improvement is much less likely. If there is no medical reason not to do so, a program of speech improvement can be begun by you.

Delayed or retarded speech, if truly serious, is often a cause of nonadmission to school. Teachers in kindergarten and the first two grades, however, will sometimes have a child in their classes whose speech is obviously less well developed than that of the other boys and girls. As has been said, the cause of such retardation may be mental deficiency or a severe hearing loss; whether or not there is such organic causation should be determined first of all. If medical examination shows nothing on either score, the cause may be emotional—in which case a psychiatric analysis should be called for. Often, however, the problem is simply the result of low motivation, or a low level of linguistic stimulation. Once the teacher is reasonably certain there is no organic or neurotic condition, the process of ear training and drill can be begun. In many cases, a classroom teacher can do much to help children improve their speech. The kind of drills you have used to develop good voice and diction in yourself are applicable, after it has once been determined definitely that there is no medical or deep-seated psychological cause for the problem.

What the teacher can do

As a nonspecialist, untrained in the specific disciplines of speech therapy, however, there are real limits upon your probable helpfulness to the child who has a severe speech handicap. Even in such cases, however, there are important things you can do.

First of all, as a teacher you can work to build within your class a feeling of "group," which truly accepts and includes all of the children in the room. You may very well have to help the child whose speech is different to learn how to make the best use of what abilities he does have. As human beings, we all have a tendency to judge ourselves *totally* inferior because of a single inferiority. The literature of psychiatry is filled with case histories of small men whose height affected their whole lives, causing them to develop all manner of complex fears and insecurities. It was, for them at least, unfortunate that our culture seemed to demand that men be "tall, dark, and handsome." In a similar fashion, it is also unfortunate that our culture seems to place such high premium upon the ability to speak. Even little children know that approval often depends upon clear speech. When they cannot seem to develop clear speech, some of them reject their *whole* selves as being unworthy. You will need to help such a child to find out what he *can* do, and to offer him objective understanding of his problem. You will need to give him sincere praise when it is merited, and to help him find areas where such sincere praise can be earned. His sense of security needs bolstering, and you can help him.

You can help him also by giving him some true perceptions of himself. Do not praise his speech if it is bad—he knows that you are being dishonest, and he probably does not want your pity. But if what he says is understandable, tell him so, and commend his efforts. Call on him as you do the others, varying his task perhaps if the clinician suggests it. But you will not help him to feel that speaking is pleasurable, nor will you help him learn to speak understandably if you take away from him all opportunity to speak. When he does speak, do not set your sights too high, and do not in any way give him the impression that you disapprove of what he does or are impatient with him.

Be careful that you and your authority do not become a threat. Of course you must work also to prevent the other children from becoming a threat either. Find out what he really needs—is it affection? Is it attention? Is it some feeling of success in something? These things you can arrange. Perhaps his greatest need is to be left alone! Handicapped children are often understandably over-protected. Remember, *your* aim for him—better speech—may not be his great "felt need" at all!

Observe the ways in which he adjusts, and help him to build acceptable social skills. Does he move toward or against his world? His speech responses will tend to follow his over-all pattern. You may need to teach him truer standards of value and judgment than just success-failure.

In general, then, regardless of the nature of the speech handicap the child has, you can help him in the following ways.

1. Insist upon expert diagnosis of his problem.
2. Create for him a feeling of security and belonging in his relationship to you and to the class.
3. Find his real needs and attempt to meet them, as well as the speech goals you feel he ought to be seeking.
4. Encourage him to speak, and help him find satisfaction in his speaking.
5. Learn all that you can about his problem. At the end of this chapter are some suggested readings, but the best source of information will be the doctor and the speech clinician working specifically with the child. It goes without saying that you will help these experts in every way possible through your regular classwork.

Whatever you do, avoid making things worse.

1. Do nothing to make the child feel inferior, self-conscious, or laughed-at because of his speech.
2. Never require him to speak better than he can.
3. Be sure that he is neither failed nor praised, penalized nor protected because of his defect.

Summary

Speech handicaps may be organic, psychological, or behavioral in their causes. Once medical examination and clinical diagnosis have determined the nature of the disorder and its probable causes, a program of therapy can be begun. If a clinician is available, the classroom teacher becomes his co-worker. If no such trained help is available, there are still important things the teacher can do and can avoid doing which will be helpful. The important thing to remember is that, your school, whether or not it has a clinician, is doing *something* about the speech handicapped child. Let your class be a source of help for him—a place where he feels accepted and respected for what he can do, rather than rejected for what he cannot.

STUDY QUESTIONS

1. What is the first thing a teacher can and should do to help the child in his class who has a serious speech problem?

2. In the United States today is there any school system where help in speech correction is totally unavailable?

3. A qualified speech therapist is certified by whom?

4. Explain the nature of the speech disorders caused by cleft palate, cerebral palsy, a severe hearing loss, and mental retardation.

5. What seems to be the relationship between anxiety and stuttering?

6. What are the commonest of all speech defects? How can you go about helping your students develop clearer speech if there is no medical reason not to do so?

7. How can the classroom teacher help a speech-handicapped child in his class?

8. Why must the child develop objective understanding of his problem? How can you help him develop it?

9. What should the teacher avoid doing in order not to make a child's defect even worse?

10. What is meant by the statement that your school, whether or not it has a clinician, is doing *something* about the speech handicapped child?

SUGGESTED CLASS ACTIVITIES

1. Discuss together:

   1) How can the speech handicapped child be identified? How serious must a speech deviation be before it is considered as clinical?

2) In what ways could you as a classroom teacher help a speech therapist in diagnosis and therapy?

3) What is the relationship between speech defects and social maladjustment?

4) Why should the classroom teacher consult a specialist concerning serious cases of speech deviation?

2. While it is true that you cannot really appreciate the psychological barrier to speech that is felt by the speech defective unless you are yourself a speech handicapped person, you can project yourself somewhat into the tension he feels every time he opens his mouth to speak. Go to a drugstore where you do not ordinarily trade, and order coffee or a "coke," pretending that you are a stutterer. Afterwards, analyze your feelings. What did you fear? Why? (As an undergraduate attempting this assignment, I went into four stores before I "made it!") This simple exercise will give you real insight. Notice that you not only hesitate to speak, but—having in a sense established that you are a "stutterer," you will probably keep on "stuttering" while you talk to the fountain clerk. Talk your experience over in class.

SUPPLEMENTARY MATERIAL

Eisenson, Jon, and Mardel Ogilvie, *Speech Correction in the Schools,* New York: The Macmillan Company, 1957. This fine book includes helpful sections dealing with all of the difficulties discussed in this chapter. For each there are lengthy bibliographies of additional materials, and concerning each there is a brief suggestion of what the ordinary classroom teacher can do. Read especially Chapter XIV, "Speech Correction Services."

13

Helping those who already have good speech skill

From time to time there will appear in your classes a student who has really superior speaking abilities. In conversation, in recitation, in discussion, he will have a power of expression and fluency which the others will not have. Such a student needs careful guidance in his development, and he should, of course, be steered into whatever speech courses and activities your school affords.

Most of his training, however, will not occur in these specialized situations, but in his daily classwork and social life. In other words, if he becomes merely glib, or conceited, or fails in some other way to make the best possible use of his aptitudes and skills, the speech teacher alone is not responsible. Unfortunately for any hopes you may have of ducking your responsibilities, it is a fact that whatever such a student does with his skill is of great importance to all of us. Consider our society. It is democratic in government, with its business life competitive and based upon persuasive selling. It lives and moves on talk. Even our social activities are highly organized into clubs and other groups in which speech plays a major role. We live, in other words, in what is essentially a world of talk—a world in which the able man who can speak well moves ahead into positions of importance in government, in business, and in community and social life. Speech skill is necessary—as a nation we must prize the students who develop it, for they will almost inevitably be among our leaders.

Special problems

Prior to the specific development of any instructional program there must be a consideration of purposes and goals. The aims of education have been varyingly defined, and there is no real agreement upon which definition is the most useful. No matter how these aims are phrased, however, they will include some recognition of "preparing" for the "good life," as well as some practical suggestion of professional training. In other words, the good teacher must consider the individual needs of each pupil, both as a human being and as a potentially self-supporting person. As we have already shown, the speech handicapped present certain specialized problems in both of these areas. The problems presented by the gifted in speech are of quite a different nature, of course, but they are equally real and deserve our thoughtful attention. Because such a student is good, however, the teacher is likely to give him less attention than the others in the class. This tendency is unfortunate, for he actually deserves as much or more attention than anyone else, rather than less, because of his potential role of leadership.

Many times already we have pointed out that speech is an aspect of human behavior. This simple statement, however, has many complex overtones, for human behavior is not simple. For example, the high school age student with obvious oral skill may be, in terms of his total behavior patterns, either outgoing or withdrawn.

He may, to oversimplify, in some cases have his skill because of an effort to compensate for shortcomings, whether real or imaginary. On the other hand, he may have the skill because he has a strong liking for people and a desire to share ideas and experiences with them—or it may be that he has no dominant urge to communicate in his make-up, but has, instead, been trained through an articulate, sociable family life to express himself freely and cogently at will. All those who speak well, in other words, are not the same kind of people, and they do not speak well because of the same reasons. Various analyses of speech skill in relationship with other abilities have turned up almost no clearly positive correlations. With the possible exception of a relatively high general intelligence, and a fairly high level of social adjustment, we cannot assume anything about a pupil simply because he can speak well.* In fact, we have learned historically that all kinds of men can sway multitudes. Speaking, in other words, is essentially nonmoral in that it can be used for good or for ill.

Writing many centuries ago, Quintilian defined the great orator as a good man, skilled in speaking, speaking truth. If we accept this definition, our obligation as teachers becomes clear. When we find a person who has already intuitively or consciously developed skill in speaking, we should provide him with truth, and help him become a good man.

For example, can we give more time to discussion? Can we work more with group projects, and provide opportunities for our students who want to learn more than the minimum? What better way is there to widen horizons than through a lively exchange of ideas? As teachers we must challenge our more vocal students,

* See Howard Gilkinson, "Experimental and Statistical Research in General Speech," *Quarterly Journal of Speech,* 30, No. 1 (Feb. 1944), pp. 98-100. See also Edward John Joseph Kramar, "The Relationships of the Wechsler-Bellvue and A.C.E. Intelligence Tests with Performance Scores in Speaking and the Brown-Carlson Listening Comprehension Test" (Doctoral Dissertation, Florida State University, 1955), and Joe M. Ball, "An Experimental Study of the Relationship Between the Ability to Impart Information Orally and the Primary Mental Abilities, Verbal Comprehension and General Reasoning" (Doctoral Dissertation, University of Southern California, 1951).

and keep them thinking, so the obligatory relationship between the ability to talk and the necessity of having something to say will become second nature.

We can inculcate the good man aspect in a number of ways, not the least of which is our own example. Integrity does not magically appear; it must be carefully developed and nurtured. It is easy to be tempted to call on the good speaker too often. But this is potentially dangerous because of the egotism it can foster. The essential purpose of speaking, after all, is communication, not display. It is more important that the skills of discussion, of conversation, and of public speaking be developed than the skills of oratory or declamation. Speaking is an overt act, and actions have consequences. The consequences of skillful speaking are measures of the integrity of the speaker.

In other words, the possession of skill somehow brings its own problems. The young, immature student suddenly discovers that he has power. He can use it to get his way. He can talk his parents out of things, he can "feed the girls a line," he can sell more tickets to the school play than anyone, he can "pull the wool over his teacher's eyes." These are tempting vistas! Even though we be educational pragmatists, some old-fashioned idealism is needed at this point. The essential goodness of a man cannot be measured alone by his effectiveness in gaining his ends. The student who has real speaking skill must somehow be taught that there is more to his responsibility than success in getting what he wants.

What the teacher can do

Speech is essentially a useful art, and its purposes are mainly utilitarian. In the pre-school and primary years the teacher's main speech objective with the child who has good speech will be to help him learn to use it for cooperative endeavor. There are numbers of ways in which the integrative values of speaking can be emphasized. For example, the child can be taught the importance of certain social niceties such as etiquette and manners, which have an oral side and are a part of interacting with others.

Informal dramatizations and the playing of oral games will also stimulate teamwork. Telling times, oral reading, the bearing of messages—all of these are oral experiences in which the child with good speech can share rather than display his abilities.

As the child grows somewhat older, class recitation and discussion come into the picture, as will clubs and committees. In these situations the child with effective speech will become a leader almost without fail. Your job as his teacher is to help him keep his perspective, to counsel away his bossiness, and to instill in him a sincere sense of thoughtfulness for others. Even in the early grades, children are old enough to begin the use of simple parliamentary forms, and can be depended upon for important committee work concerning such necessary classroom details as meeting guests, passing milk and straws, conducting short daily devotionals, leading the flag salute, and so on. Change officers and committees frequently, and be especially sure that the child with skill has an opportunity to perform a variety of tasks.

When the child is in junior high school, or senior high school, you should bend every effort to get him into dramatics, debate, forensics, and the like—or into speech classes if your school offers them. But even here you cannot resign what is essentially your job. You must continue to help the student who is good in speech to develop his fund of ideas, his respect for evidence, and his personal integrity.

Specifically, suggestions such as the following are important guideposts for working with students of established ability in speech.

1. Insist upon high standards of content and thought in all that such a student says. It is easy for him to bluff his way. You must give close attention to *what* he says, insisting upon accuracy and clear organization. Since the thing will be said well, it will be listened to. All the more reason to emphasize what is said. The "gift of gab" is an empty gift.
2. Stress the collaborative aspects of speaking and encourage participation in contest situations only within the context of "doing one's best" and "profiting from the experience." It is nice to win prizes, but the real purpose of speaking is to influence others. Because a

student can get what he wants, he often loses sight of the necessity of working within the framework of the group.

3. Teach the student to respect the power of words. Truth and fantasy must be separated. Tale-bearing must be discouraged and other disintegrative aspects of talking such as name-calling, sarcasm, the use of unsupported assertions, and the like, must be curbed. Under no circumstances should a student be permitted to substitute shrewdness for thought, strategy for interaction. "Making the worse appear the better cause" does not mark real speech ability, because the words are irresponsible and the ideas, in the long run, are demonstrably invalid.

4. Do not exploit the child's ability. No school, no teacher, no parent should ever be permitted to win glory at the expense of a personality. The conflict is not necessary, however, for there are ways to stress personal development and let winning become incidental. When a person is good and consistently does his best, his share of "wins" will come automatically.

Summary

The child who has developed a high level of speech ability should be encouraged to participate in as much of the formal speech and speech activities programs of the school as he possibly can. What underlies speech skill will vary from person to person. Because of the importance of this skill in our way of life, it should be analyzed and encouraged in the classroom by all teachers as much as possible. Even though these individual differences do exist, the teacher should set especially high standards of content for all such students, and should stress the group cooperation aspects of speech, teaching the student especially to respect the power of words.

STUDY QUESTIONS

1. Why is the statement, "Good speakers are born," inaccurate?

2. Why should the classroom teacher give special consideration to the problems of a student who has superior speaking skills?

3. What are some possible causes of the development of speech skill?

4. With what other abilities, aptitudes, or general personality characteristics does speech skill seem to correlate?

5. How did Quintilian define an orator? What about this definition today?

6. How can a teacher help a student who is good in speech to develop into an especially useful citizen?

7. Why is it potentially dangerous to push the student with skill into "show-off" experiences?

8. What is meant by the statement that speech is a useful art? How does a useful art differ from a fine art? From a science?

9. What is the main speech teaching job of the teacher so far as the child who already has skill is concerned?

10. Is the training of the speech of such a child the exclusive province of the speech teacher? Why do you answer as you do?

SUGGESTED CLASS ACTIVITIES

1. Think back over the speech training available in the schools which you attended. Write a short paper in which you 1) describe exactly what was offered, as nearly as you can recall it, 2) speculate as to the probable aim and motivation of each part of the program or activity, and 3) evaluate its usefulness in developing the speech of a student who was already good. Bring your papers to class and pool your conclusions. Would you say that the situation these analyses summarize was good?

2. Discuss in class:

1) What are the usual characteristics of a truly gifted child? Is effective oral skill usually one of these characteristics?

2) Why does the gifted child require special attention from the teacher?

3) Are all contests bad? Or is the problem one of how contests are used?

SUPPLEMENTARY MATERIAL

Backus, Ollie L., *Speech in Education,* New York: Longmans, Green and Company, 1943, pp. 1-28, "What is the Place of Speech in Education," and pp. 236-312, "Applied Speech." Although these pages do not apply completely to the problem of teaching the child who has superior speech ability, they do much to place this part of the total task of teaching in a meaningful context.

14

Speech can and should be taught by every teacher

Have you ever stopped to think how much time you spend speaking and listening? Compare that amount of time with what you spend reading and writing—or doing sums. It is apparent after even casual consideration that there can be no real comparison. Even the best educated of us sometimes go weeks without adding, subtracting, multiplying, or dividing *anything!* We often go hours on end without picking up a pencil, or reading a word. But we are rarely silent. In fact, if we are isolated or left alone even for a short time, we talk to ourselves, or to imaginary companions. Speech, then, is basic. It fills definite life-needs for man—the gregarious animal. A deaf-mute has a difficult time adjusting to society; but an illiterate can and often does live happily and contentedly among his fellow-men without ever being recognized as such.

Speech can be taught

Speech is not clearly an art or a science, like music or biology. It is not even entirely a skill, like English composition or playing the trombone. It is not exclusively a professional field, like plumbing, or medicine or the ministry. Yet it is all of these things at once—an art, a science, a skill, a professional field—all of them, and yet none of them. It involves *knowing*, as does a science, and *doing*, as does an art. It improves with study and practice as a skill, and there are definite professional standards applicable to it. It ranges from the creative artistry of the theatre, to the scientific method of the speech therapist; from the esthetic beauty of a skillful oral interpreter, to the shrewd, hard logic of a skillful debater; from the learned research of the voice scientist to the friendly intuitiveness of the teacher who would encourage first graders in story-telling or impromptu dramatics.

Speech, in other words, is not a narrow academic discipline. It cannot be easily classified, for it is not readily identifiable as a skill, or a fine art, or even as a language art. Speech, you see, is an aspect of human behavior. Moreover, speech is *learned* behavior. Every one of us has learned speech—we are living, breathing proof that speech can be taught.

We know that the halting speech of the boy who stutters, the agonizingly painful speech of the child with cerebral palsy, and the lisping speech of the adolescent high school girl can all be changed, with guidance, into more acceptable, more understandable patterns of speech behavior. Scientific studies have shown that training in public speaking can make high school students better able to impress boards of judges representing a wide variety of adult occupations. We know that, in many cases, training in speech has resulted in desirable personality changes, and in more satisfactory social adjustments. In other words, we *know* that speech is an aspect of human behavior. We *know* that it is a learned activity. We *know* that good training can affect it in ways that are positive and desirable.

The assumption that speech can be taught, then, seems today to have general acceptance. The problem is not, can it be taught— but should it be!

Speech should be taught

Let us return to the original question about the relative amount of time spent in speaking and listening. Many authorities believe that thought itself is sub-vocal speech*—that most of our successful social experiences are the result of good speech—that speech not only reflects, but in some senses even determines personality. We know that speech is a valuable means of self-expression—a safety valve for the pressures of our time. We "speak our mind," "talk it out," and "just have to tell somebody" almost daily. We know that our primary personal means of communication is through speech—consider the staggering number of telephones, radio stations, and TV cables which are hypothesized upon this as fact. And speech, too, is our most direct means of influencing the society about us to behave as we wish. Rare indeed is the parent who does not on some occasion threaten his three-year-old with a "good talking to" if he does not eat his breakfast!

Can there be any real doubt that any aspect of human behavior so common, so vital, so often badly used, should be an *integral* part of the training offered by our schools?

Why is it that so many schools make no effort whatever to help their pupils increase their abilities in speech, while almost all insist upon hours of instruction in theme writing, and the reading of literature? Most students today learn driving, or sewing, or cooking, or woodworking; they study the finer points of basketball, or baseball, or modern dance. On the other hand, they learn little or nothing in any orderly or guided way about the human activity of speech, which is directly related to almost every single thing they will ever do. Why is this, and what can be done?

* This idea is developed by Sapir, Bloomfield, deLaguna, and others. Probably one of its fullest statements (and certainly an interesting one) is found in Benjamin Whorf, *Language, Thought, and Reality* (The Technical Press of Massachusetts Institute of Technology, 1956).

Every teacher a speech teacher

Consider how you learned to speak. First of all, you learned by experience. In some fashion, when you were an infant, you learned that certain sounds would get certain results. A little later you learned by imitation, consciously making the sounds you heard others make. Still later, perhaps even in adulthood, you learned more speech skills as a result of deliberately gained insight, as has been the case in this class.

Are there such strange processes that you cannot and will not use them in your own classes? Certainly not. As a teacher, you will undoubtedly create situations in your classroom which will in and of themselves stimulate speech. Such situations encourage the first kind of learning. You will also find that your own speech operates as a model for your pupils. This kind of learning is of the second type. With very little extra effort, you can even offer guidance in the speech development of your pupils—the third type of speech training.

Think back over what you have been studying. Do you not think that you could help a student develop a better voice, just as you have done? Develop better diction, as you have? Develop more expressiveness, a better presence, better gestures? Could you not help him develop his ideas and organize them? Do you not feel that you could help a student improve his reading, his story-telling, his expository speaking, his conversation, his discussion leadership and participation? Of course you are not an expert, but do you not feel that you could now do *something* which would be helpful?

Speech training is not a "frill," it is basic to all learning, and to all teaching. Of course you are not an expert. Let us all grant that you could not necessarily put on a good play or coach debate. Let us grant that you may not be qualified to prescribe therapy for a speech-handicapped child. But, as a classroom teacher, you can and must do a great many things simply because you cannot avoid them. You will talk, and your students will listen; they will talk, and you will listen. Why not give these processes some additional thought, and add to them some things which will begin (or continue) the speech growth of your pupils.

Summary

To teach speech is to teach people. Listen to your pupils. This must come first. What are their problems? Are there any speech handicapped in the group? Are there any who seem gifted in speech? When your first over-all, general analysis is complete, make a specific analysis of each child. Listen to his first oral performance in class, and observe him also in conversation.

1. Is his voice pleasant? Suitably pitched? Adequately loud? Well-resonated? Is his rate too fast or too slow?
2. What about his diction—is it clear and understandable? Does he slight consonants? Distort vowels? Has he a pronounced dialect?
3. Is he expressive?
4. Is he poised?
5. Can he handle ideas effectively? Has he something to say? Does he treat speech responsibly? Can his materials be relied upon?

When your objective diagnosis is finished, outline a few simple projects designed to secure improvement. The kinds of projects you have been doing in this class may offer a suggestion of some ways in which you can make speech training a part of your classroom activity. Other suggestions can be found in the books listed in the Supplementary Material section at the end of each chapter.

Among the principal aims of education should undoubtedly be the development of skill in communication of all kinds, and especially development in speech. The United States in particular badly needs to awaken to the fundamental importance of speech training for her school children, and for her high school and college young people. Speech is the whole person. It is relevant to his needs, reflective of his self, and his principal means of interaction with his world. It is impossible for a teacher to do nothing about the speech of his pupils. Even in doing nothing, he does something.

STUDY QUESTIONS

1. In what ways is speech an art?
2. In what ways is speech a skill?
3. Give two or three examples which would seem to indicate that speech is a learned activity.
4. What is a possible relationship between speech and thought? Between our speech and our personality?
5. What are the three principal ways in which our speech is learned?
6. In what sense is every teacher a speech teacher?
7. What is the first general analysis which you should make of your class, before you begin to plan any speech-related work with them?
8. What specific points should you analyze in planning speech-related lessons and activities?
9. Why has the United States special reasons for concern about speech training in our educational system?
10. What is meant by the statement that "to do nothing is to do something" about teaching speech?

SUGGESTED CLASS ACTIVITIES

1. Assume that you are teaching. Determine the grade-level you propose to teach, or—if you are aiming at the secondary schools—choose your specific subject. Plan two assignments which you might give early in the term, which would permit you at the same time to make some speech analysis.

2. Suggest assignments suitable in this same general situation which might be a part of your regular class outline, but which might also teach something about: 1) the use of the voice, 2) the clarity of diction, 3) expressiveness, 4) gesture and presence, 5) content materials and their ordering.

SUPPLEMENTARY MATERIAL

Fessenden, Seth, *Speech and the Teacher*, New York: Longmans, Green and Company, Inc., 1946, Chapter Four, "Teaching with Speech" and Chapter Five, "The Teacher and the Student's Speech." These chapters, while already somewhat dated, are nevertheless filled with good ideas.

Index